Critical Condition

The Lack of Common Sense in America

Kevin Turnbaugh

WestBow
PRESS
A DIVISION OF THOMAS NELSON

Copyright © 2011 Kevin Turnbaugh

All rights reserved. No part of this book may be used or reproduced by any means, graphic, electronic, or mechanical, including photocopying, recording, taping or by any information storage retrieval system without the written permission of the publisher except in the case of brief quotations embodied in critical articles and reviews.

WestBow Press books may be ordered through booksellers or by contacting:

WestBow Press
A Division of Thomas Nelson
1663 Liberty Drive
Bloomington, IN 47403
www.westbowpress.com
1-(866) 928-1240

Because of the dynamic nature of the Internet, any web addresses or links contained in this book may have changed since publication and may no longer be valid. The views expressed in this work are solely those of the author and do not necessarily reflect the views of the publisher, and the publisher hereby disclaims any responsibility for them.

Any people depicted in stock imagery provided by Thinkstock are models, and such images are being used for illustrative purposes only.

Certain stock imagery © Thinkstock.

ISBN: 978-1-4497-1574-8 (sc)
ISBN: 978-1-4497-1575-5 (dj)
ISBN: 978-1-4497-1573-1 (e)

Library of Congress Control Number: 2011926677

Printed in the United States of America

WestBow Press rev. date: 4/25/2011

This book has been written to honor all Americans who utilize common sense in their everyday lives, give praise to God Almighty, cherish the rights and freedoms accorded to us in the Constitution, and show love and respect to their neighbors.

Also, to all of the men and women who serve in the US Army (USA), US Navy (USN), US Air Force (USAF), US Marine Corps (USMC), and the US Coast Guard (USCG) who keep us free and safe, especially those who paid the ultimate price to allow us the freedoms we have in the United States.

Contents

Preface	ix
Introduction	xi
Chapter 1—Big Government vs. John and Jane Q. Public	1
Chapter 2—Energy Is Just Blowing in the Wind	7
Chapter 3—Dividing Issues	13
Chapter 4—See You in Court	27
Chapter 5—Getting Rid of Christ in Our Country	35
Chapter 6—Using the Military to Defend Our Borders	39
Chapter 7—Private vs. Public Health Care	45
Chapter 8—Short and Simple	49
Chapter 9—The Media Nonsense	53
Chapter 10—If You Don't Vote, Don't Complain	57
Chapter 11—A Mosque near "Ground Zero"	61
Chapter 12—The Immigration Issue	65
Chapter 13—Wake Up, People of the World	69
Chapter 14—It Is Spelled with a C	81
Conclusion— A Common-Sense Idea	87
Acknowledgement	89
References	91

Preface

This book has been written for several reasons, but the most important one is that I truly believe there is a disease in our country that is preventing people from using common sense. I am convinced that the United States is in critical condition, and we need to get common sense back into our government on the federal, state, and local levels very soon. The use of common sense has been replaced by bureaucracy, political correctness, and the fear that we may offend people if we do not treat them with kid gloves.

Today, you cannot get a straight answer from a member of Congress, the president, or most government leaders to save your life. They have no idea how to simply say yes or no. However, in a different way, they do not understand the word no when it comes to the people voting against something the social progressives (more like regressives, in my opinion) want, like legalizing marijuana or health insurance benefits for same-sex partners. The voters say no, so they just go to the courts, and the judges make law from the bench and overrule the voters.

In this book, I will look at several of these issues, doing my best to be fair, yet letting you know my opinion on each subject. In addition, we will utilize common sense in looking at these issues and why they are just plain nutty ideas, stupid, or totally wrong. All Scripture references in this book are from the New International Version (NIV), or the King James Version (KJV).

—Kevin Turnbaugh

Introduction

I do not think anything is in more need of a good, healthy checkup in our country than the use of common sense. The United States is full of college graduates who cannot read worth a lick and have no idea what it means to think something out but parade around with their degrees as if they are the best thing walking on the street. Then you have the know nothings who cannot even spell common sense and would not know what to do with it if they had it in their possession. The worst thing is that the two types of people I have just described are running our country today.

We have three components to our government, and none of them can spell common sense. The first is the executive branch, which includes the president and vice-president, the White House staffers, the Cabinet members, and those useless czars. Next is the legislative branch, which is made up of the Congress and staffers. Finally, we have the judicial branch and the many judges who seem to think they can make law from the bench.

After these folks come the organizations that continually try to force Americans to change things to their way of thinking. They raise their voices, claiming their civil rights are being denied, just because they do not get their way all of the time. The opposite side of this coin is those in America who just sit back and literally do nothing. They depend on welfare to pay for their food and want public health care but won't lift a finger to get a job and try to improve themselves.

Between these two kinds of people are those who bust their rear ends every day, pay most of the taxes, and give the most to charity. They seem to always get the raw end of the deal when trying to make a better life for themselves and their families.

We are going to address several of the issues that some are just messing up. They are failing to use their heads when dealing with the issues and mainly have no idea how to use common sense in resolving the issues. Instead of just charging ahead into a wall, we need to stop and think about turning one way or the other to avoid the wall. Putting a little thought into a subject, dilemma, or serious situation will bring about a quick resolution that works. However, if we just keep running into the wall and give no thought to why it hurts when we hit it, we will get nowhere in this country but down the drain.

We will look at each issue individually. We will brainstorm it, dissect it, and try to come up with some kind of idea or suggestions to resolve the issue. These will be my thoughts and opinions, but I will do my best to look at each one fairly. Every issue has more than one side, so we will try to address each side of an argument. However, where common sense comes in best is when the obvious answer is in front of us and there is no need to discuss any options.

What really steams me about people today is that they deal with an issue, a problem, or a situation in ways that do not do anything about solving it in a sensible manner. Although this happens everywhere, this way of dealing with the issues of our country is most prevalent in our Congress. Instead of a dog-and-pony show, we have a donkey-and-elephant show, and the mixture is just ridiculous. I am reminded of a sign we had hanging in the Freeman Shoe Factory in Hanover, Pennsylvania, that describes our government today perfectly. It said, "Getting things done around here is like mating elephants. It is done with a lot of hollering and screaming. It is done on a high level, and it takes two years to see results."

The truth is that our whole country is like our Congress and government officials. We are so divided on issues that there is no common ground, no way of coming to an agreement, and no plan to resolve the issues. We want it our way, and if you don't like it, then you are wrong. We get like little kids who want their way. We throw tantrums, raise the roof about not getting our way, and demand the courts rule in our favor. All this does is tear our country farther apart at the seams.

The last time this country came together in a common cause was just after the attacks of September 11, 2001. For a few weeks, we were Americans and patriots, and we were cheering on the president when he went after the Islamic terrorist organizations that attacked our land in such a cowardly way. Before this, you would have to go all the way back to World War II to find such patriotism among our country and people. It is sad that a tragedy like 9/11 or the attack on Pearl Harbor has to occur to bring us together as Americans. Let's get some common sense back in this place.

Chapter 1

Big Government vs. John and Jane Q. Public

The modern Tea Party movement takes its name and attitude toward our government from the patriots who threw that first Tea Party in Boston, Massachusetts just before the war for independence. They were fed up with being told they had to pay taxes to the king of England without having representation on the decision to levy the taxes. So what did they do? They literally pitched the tea overboard in this case. They wanted to be heard, be represented, and have a say in what was or was not done in and around them.

Like King George III, our current governmental leaders are turning a deaf ear to what the people are saying. The Congress we had before the elections in November of 2010, and even the current Congress, has members that have their own agendas and could not care less what the folks at home are saying, shouting, and writing to them. The biggest issue that Congress had was that they had no concern about running up a debt that we can never repay. This is just plain fiscally irresponsible, but they did not give a good rip what we thought or did not like about their actions.

On every issue, bill, or problem that comes before Congress, one side always has to blame the other for it even existing. I can remember when the Congress was stomping their feet about Reaganomics, but the truth is recorded in history, President Reagan's economic plans helped a sluggish country become very prosperous and fiscally sound. Even President Clinton's balancing of the budget on several occasions came about by dealing with the issues, what was causing the problems, and then making the hard choices for the good of the country. But not today! It is spend, spend, spend, and spend some more, and we will worry about paying the bill later.

If history is a good teacher of what is to come, and it is, later will never come. The fiscal irresponsibility of our government today is on a downhill slide straight into a major depression that will make the stock market crash, and subsequent Great Depression, in October 1929 look like a little hiccup. I don't know how many times President Barack Obama has blamed the financial problems today on President George W. Bush's administration. But the truth is that most of the problems today he brought on himself by demanding that the health care bill pass that will cost more than it will save, if anything. On top of that, he wants to hand out money like it is coming from a candy factory to keep things going.

Then you have the Obama administration acting like bullies in a school play yard and telling people and states that they must do it their way only. The stupid response to the Arizona immigration law is a perfect example of this bullying. First, the president told the attorney general to get tough with Arizona, so he went before Congress about this new law and criticized it for causing potential racial profiling. Then under questioning by the members of the Congressional hearing, he admitted that he had not even read the law. What a hypocrite!

If you are going to attack something or someone, you need to know what you are talking about. Obviously the attorney general does not know how to spell common sense or use it either. But he is definitely not alone on this lack of using common sense. That health care bill I spoke about was over two thousand five hundred pages; it is filled with hidden regulations and says absolutely nothing. Just like going from one place to another using a straight line, the same should be used in our laws, legislation, and so on. Say it plainly, clearly, and simply so all can understand it, work with it, and fulfill it in our everyday life. I guess that makes too much sense, so they cannot do it that way!

We the people, the common folk, have to keep to our budgets within our financial means in everything we do, but this is not so in our government. What, we have run out of money? Well print some more! Sure, that is the quick fix, but who is going to pay for our fourteen trillion dollar plus–debt in the future? At the same time, we are buying friends around the world by handing out money like we have it growing on trees. If we would not give out any foreign aid for one budget year, we would put a major dent in our deficit but have no friends. If we have to buy our friends, what kind of friends are they?

Then there are our income tax laws, the lobbyists, and the major loopholes in the laws. I am no mathematical whiz, but use of the old Keep It Simple Stupid (KISS) method should be utilized. However, the government strikes again. Between members of Congress wanting this or that in or out of the law and the lobbyists working on keeping their interests deductions in the laws, you end up with a total mess from the information you put in block 1 to the block where you sign it before sending it in for what you hope will be a refund. The tax laws of our nation are a perfect example of a lack of common sense in our government. First, they are so confusing that without a certified public accountant (CPA), you may have a hard time determining if a deduction applies to you or not. Further, you may need the assistance of a lawyer to understand the wording in the laws. The problem here is that most of us are neither a CPA nor a lawyer or may have difficulty affording one or the other, so why are the tax laws so confusing? Well, let me put forth a possible resolution.

In the county where my wife and I live in Pennsylvania, Adams County, we have a local income tax of 1.5 percent of your gross income. The tax is simple, easy to understand, and takes about fifteen to thirty minutes to do, including sealing the envelope and placing a stamp on it for mailing. The form asks for your gross income (wages, tips, and the like). Next you list the amount of taxes you paid in over the past year. Then you take your income and multiply it by .015 to find out what your tax burden is to the county. The difference is what you owe or get in a refund; however, most of the time the numbers come out to less than a dollar (which is waived). You sign and date the form and mail it and you're done. This is a perfect example of the KISS method.

With this method of taxing, all pay their fair share, and you will not need tax professionals to help you fill them in and prepare them for the Internal Revenue Service (IRS). I think you would also find that the IRS could be drastically downsized with this simple tax form as well, saving our government even more money. In addition, with today's home computers, everybody would be able to fill in the form and send it in electronically, saving the IRS and the government even more. Add to this all of the printing of forms and publications that would no longer be needed and all of those IRS offices across the country that we could close, saving even more money for the government. This comes from a simple person who does not even have a college degree.

Then there is an even simpler method of taxing, and almost every state has this one. Instead of an income tax, we would change over to a National Sales Tax (NST) on everything bought by consumers. If the federal government would establish a 5 percent sales tax on all services, goods, and anything sold at a retail price, the government would get five cents for every dollar in sales. There would be no more income tax deductions from your paycheck, no more tax-deferred insurance and 401K stuff. You would be able to keep it all, and as you buy things (food, cars, television sets, homes, and so on), the government would get five cents for every dollar spent.

I know that several states have both sales tax and income tax, but the thing here is that the more consumers have in their pockets, the more they will probably spend. Even if between the federal and state governments they would establish a 15 percent sales tax, we the consumers would still be ahead of the game from what we have now. Some of us are paying more than 30 percent in federal income taxes, so a 15 percent sales tax would be cutting our tax burden in half. You do not have to be a rocket scientist to know that you will have more money to spend using this method.

The savings to our federal and state governments would be in the millions of dollars every year. The IRS could be eliminated for the most part, as well as the state revenue offices, and all of the buildings and any other overhead involved would be greatly reduced, if not totally eliminated. Yeah, I know that would put a lot of people out of work. Maybe, but maybe not! With more money in the marketplace, that would mean more jobs and opportunities for expanding small businesses. About the only people who would really be hurt here would be the CPA's, tax services companies, and those who process the tax forms sent in each year. Well that may be cold on my part, but something is going to have to give soon when we are looking at a fourteen trillion–dollar plus deficit, with no way to pay for it in the near future.

I have just dealt with income taxes so far, but we could look at other areas too. In the 1950's, then-President Dwight Eisenhower signed the Interstate Highway Bill that created our country's highway system that we have today. Just think if we still had those old two-lane roads (like the famous Route 66) to get everywhere on and no interstate roads. Well, to maintain these and other roads, the federal government adds taxes to every gallon of gas sold, and I believe this is a good tax. Otherwise, every road would be a toll road. Then there are the taxes established on what are referred to as sin taxes. Liquor and tobacco products are taxed heavily, and these taxes should stay in place too. When people sit down and brainstorm an issue, options that can lead to large savings can be the result. Just look at what we have discussed in these few pages alone. The savings in labor, building, and other costs is several million per year, at least. All it took was a little common sense.

Chapter 2

Energy Is Just Blowing in the Wind

As I am writing this chapter, our nation is dealing with the worst environmental disaster in the Gulf of Mexico from the oil rig explosion on a British Petroleum (BP) oil drilling platform. From the time of the actual explosion until they capped the leak, it was estimated that well over one million barrels of oil leaked into the Gulf of Mexico.

I want to make it clear at this point that I favor offshore drilling of oil. If it is there, go get it, in my opinion. What happened on the BP platform has not been positively established yet, but it had to have been human error or just plain cutting corners to save money. We have great technical knowhow, and if used properly, this type of accident will be just that, an accident.

The environmentalists in our country scream every time someone even suggests drilling in a new place. Yet they still put gas in their cars and would be the first ones to yell about no gas at the pumps. These dimwits want everything their way, but they do not know what their way is or how to get there. They have been yelling, stomping their feet, hollering at politicians, and have many in Congress supporting their opposition to future drilling offshore or in new land locations like in Alaska. What you do not hear from them is that except for the Exxon Valdez accident in Prince William Sound, Alaska, in

1989 and the recent BP oil spill in the Gulf, oil drilling has been quite safe.

Another issue about oil production in our country is that we could produce much more than we do, and this goes back to us buying friends around the world. In the small town of Lulling, Texas, there is so much oil there you can smell it by just driving through the town. However, the oil fields are not running anywhere near capacity. Why, you say? Well, if we stop buying oil from Middle East countries, we lose our friends. In my opinion, *tough!* If we have the oil, pump it!

There has been so much discussion (and that is putting it mildly) about opposing drilling in the Alaskan Wildlife Reserve (ANWR), even though scientists estimate that there is enough oil in that area to support our country for ten years by itself. They give no thought to the very safe record the oil fields in Barrows, Alaska, have had and that of the Alaskan Oil Pipeline.

So what is the common sense issue here? The people in the Middle East, and other countries too, who sell our country oil are polluted with money. They are making billions from us and are laughing all the way to the bank. Why are we making them rich? Let's pump our own oil and let them swim in their oil. Just think of the money our country could put toward our deficit with a simple sales tax structure applied even to gas sales at the pump, and it is our oil. As long as we depend on overseas oil, we are hurting our economy, taking away from our independence to other sources of energy, and reducing our ability to be the great nation we can be in the world.

One more thing on this issue: we need to remember that oil is not an endless commodity. Somewhere under that ground, or under that oil pool in the sea, is a bottom. Once the oil is gone, it is gone. So we need to look at other sources of energy available to us today. The use of bio-fuels and running cars on hydrogen are two that come to mind. I like the hydrogen idea because it helps in more than one way. Hydrogen is everywhere, we know it works, and the only byproduct we get from it is water. Not only did we deal with a fuel situation, but we dealt with the pollution issue too.

Here in Pennsylvania, and in neighboring states like West Virginia and others, we have great amounts of coal reserves. Coal is our nation's greatest resource, and its benefits are many. We power our electric producing plants, we make our steel in the blast furnaces, and we warm our homes. Technology today has made great strides in helping to prevent pollution from coal burning. If we abandon coal as an energy source, we are just shooting ourselves in the foot.

Another source of energy we cannot just dismiss is solar energy. The sun is a great source of energy when harnessed correctly. Our space program powers the International Space Station (ISS) by use of solar panels that convert the sun's rays into electrical energy. Many use solar panels to heat their water, generate electricity, and so on. I believe this is a source of energy we have not even scratched the surface of yet in our country, and we need to expand this research at our university and government labs.

However, the most available source of energy today blows past us every day. It is the wind, and this is not a new concept. Remember the old farms of long ago, and every one of them had a windmill for pumping water from a well and creating electricity for the farm house and barns? Somewhere down the line we thought using oil, coal, or some other type of energy was more efficient. I believe we are starting to learn how wrong we were in the past.

During a vacation in 1994, my wife and I traveled to Hawaii. While on a tour of the island of Oahu, we were shown the world's largest windmill. It continually turns from the ocean breezes that affect it all of the time. What we learned from our guide was that this one windmill generates almost one-third of the power needed to power the island. It requires no fuel to make the power, the maintenance is very low cost, and the source of the energy is free from off the ocean.

Wind power is becoming a real new and possible source to help reduce our energy consumption in this country. We have some of the windiest places on earth, and no matter where you go, the wind blows. On top of mountains, it is so windy that you can hardly stand up, and that is usually all of the time. The wind on top of Mount Washington in New Hampshire blows so hard, in the winter especially, that it has caused the coldest wind chill ever recorded. If we would place wind generators all throughout our mountain ranges, the electricity created would be immeasurable. Further, the windmills do not detract from the land, even though some environmentalists will probably come up with some kind of reason or protest over their placement. We can also place them along our shorelines to catch the ocean winds that continuously blow.

More and more you hear about people placing a wind generator on their property to help with electrical costs. In fact, there is a law in Pennsylvania, and maybe in other states too, that the electric companies must buy your unused electricity if you do not use it all. Wow, what a concept—free electricity from the wind. What was common sense and needed in the past has now become a bright new idea. What I do not understand is why anyone would be against a free source of energy, whether it is from the sun, the wind, or a gas like hydrogen. But we do have those people in our country, and I feel that they are just plain idiots for opposing such sources of free, clean energy.

One other source of energy is nuclear energy. I work at the Department of Defense (DOD) depot facility in New Cumberland, Pennsylvania, just across the Susquehanna River from Harrisburg, Pennsylvania. Just down the river from us, and in clear view of the depot, are the cooling towers of Three Mile Island (TMI). This is the place where the only nuclear accident in the United States occurred in 1979. Some people joke that you can always tell if someone lives near TMI, because they always have a glow about them. However, that joke is not very funny in our area.

The truth is that this was an accident, as is suspected to be the cause of the oil rig explosion in the Gulf of Mexico. Many new regulations, safety procedures, and ways of operating a nuclear plant were learned from the TMI incident, and all of them for the good. Prior to, and ever since, we have had no problems with any nuclear plants in our country, and the only pollution we get from the cooling towers is steam. But there is the disposal of the nuclear waste. Science needs to get on the stick in their research on how to dispose of the spent nuclear rods from these facilities. Although I do not oppose nuclear energy generation, it is not my favorite. I will take the wind any day.

Then there is the last of our free sources of energy, hydroelectric dams. If you have ever seen or maybe been to the mighty Hoover Dam in Nevada, you are immediately taken with its immensity. I listened to a show on the History Channel a few years ago, on their "Modern Marvels" series that took the watchers on a tour of the Hoover Dam facility. The size of these electrical generating units inside of the dam was astounding, and what they can do and how much electricity they can make was just as astounding.

What is even more amazing about this type of electrical generating is that it also comes from a free source. The rivers of our nation have been harnessed in many ways but none more sensibly than by dams to create electricity. But again, there is a positive byproduct from these dams. In the case of Hoover Dam, it created Lake Meade, which is the source of water for Las Vegas and many other communities in the area. It is also used as a recreational area for people to come to for a vacation and afternoon fun. All it took was someone just utilizing a little common sense, and you get power, fun, and water in one undertaking.

If you take a look back at history in our country, you can see how the best ideas of today were beneficial then too. In an attempt to bring our country out of the Depression of the 1930's, then-President Franklin D. Roosevelt initiated the Civilian Conservation Corps (CCC) that put unemployed people to work building things like the

Hoover Dam, the many dams that make up the Tennessee Valley Authority (TVA), and later the bill signed into law by President Dwight Eisenhower to create the interstate highways across our nation. The common sense here was people got jobs and were able to provide for their families, and the nation as a whole benefited from the electricity generated, water reservoirs for cities, interstate highways, and so many more positive things to all of us. We need to just sit back, look at things as they are, and ask why it has to be that way. From those kinds of discussions come great ideas. Where would we be today if the Wright brothers had not made serious observations of birds flying, how they flew, and what they could do to make it possible for us to fly today?

God Almighty put a brain in our heads so we would use it for something to benefit us all. I hear it all the time, and have said it myself, that in today's world, we do not have time to stop and think about things, how they are and work, and what can be done to improve them. We just go a top speed and hope we survive the day without a heart attack, stroke, or car accident. People drive today like they are late for everything, but the only thing they will arrive at is their funerals if they do not drive sensibly. The same goes in our work places. Technology has given us computers to speed up actions and the processing of data, but the old adage of garbage in garbage out applies. The data in a computer is only as good as the information put into it by the operator. So let's take some time once in a while and look at things as they are. Let's ask ourselves how we can make it better, safer and more efficient, and save money too.

Chapter 3

Dividing Issues

Read in the Bible: Leviticus 19:17–19, Matthew 5:42–44, 19:18–20, 22:38–40, Mark 12:30–34, Luke 10:26–28, Romans 13:8–10, Galatians 5:13–15, and James 2:7–9 (NIV).

In the Bible, Jesus tells us to love our neighbor as ourselves in response to a question from the Pharisees (the Jewish leaders of the day). They had asked Him what was the greatest Commandment, and after loving God with all of our heart, soul, and mind, loving our neighbors was the second greatest commandment. However, in today's world, that is one tough thing to do. We are so polarized on so many different issues that it isn't funny. We are divided on issues from politics to abortion to displaying religious artifacts in public, and many more divisive matters. In this chapter, I will address several of these issues and give them fair hearing but give you the straight story on each of them.

Issue 1—Politics and the Voters of America

Ever since the very early days of our country, our Founding Fathers made sure that the government would answer to the people. Our rights to freedom and happiness were set in motion with the Declaration of Independence in 1776. Then these rights were expanded with the ratification of the Constitution in 1787, and the first ten amendments (known as the Bill of Rights introduced by future President James Madison in 1789) were added to the Constitution in 1791. In all things, it was the people who had the final say in the matters of the country. This is the very essence of democracy.

The writer, the reviewers, and ultimately the approvers of our Constitution set forth a way of life in the United States that would be dictated by the voters. Those who were elected by the voters were charged with utilizing the checks and balances found within the Constitution to make sure that the executive, legislative, and judicial branches of the government followed the will of the people.

In the years from the start of our country until around the time of the Depression of the 1930's, except for a few growing pains, this was the way our country worked. We had our internal differences; we fought off oppressors and even fought a civil war over slavery. Through it all, the plans of our Founding Fathers stood the test. At the end of World War I, we started to do a little regressing in our standards as a nation, in our morals and obeying of the laws of our land. Prohibition brought the time of the gangsters, speakeasies, and many other morally degrading things to our country.

Once this time came to an end, we ended up back in combat with World War II. No matter how horrible you consider that time to have been, I truly believe it brought us as a nation back into a patriotic attitude. The postwar years of President Dwight Eisenhower are still fondly looked back upon as a time of high moral standards, belief in our nations' leaders, and our love of God. Then in 1963, we took a big step downward with the Supreme Court ruling that removed prayer and Bible reading from our schools. Since this time, we have been on this downward spiral to where we are today.

What we as a nation forgot was what Jesus said was the greatest commandment. We began to not have God in the forefront of all our decisions, ways of dealing with moral regression, and many more deteriorating activities. Instead, we decided to remove God from the very place where our future leaders are educated. Our educational standards were high at that time. We were a powerful force in the world as a nation and were respected as such by many other countries. Now our schools are full of kids who have no respect for their teachers, the moral standards hardly exist, and some schools don't even recite the Pledge of Allegiance at the beginning of the school day for fear that someone may be offended by it in some way.

All three branches of our government can take blame for the regression of our educational standards today. Our education department (part of the executive branch) is about as useful as nothing and just regulates the schools to death. The Congress is just sitting on their fannies, and the courts of our land continue to remove more and more of God from our society.

The feeling in Washington today is that they know more than the people do, so they make decisions without caring about what the people want. This was true during the Vietnam War, when President Lyndon Johnson and Defense Secretary Robert McNamara directed the war effort from the White House. This was not just stupid; it was totally irresponsible. By the time they would read reports, discuss what to do, and then sent back the orders to the commanders, the whole situation could have, and usually had, already changed. We dealt with, and still do, this same kind of thinking in our Congress and with our current leader, President Barack Obama, in our country now.

In the recent past, two issues stand out as government interfering with the will of the people. The voters spoke, but because one person or part of society did not like the result, the judicial part of our country decided to make law from the bench. First, the voters of Colorado voted overwhelmingly to deny insurance benefits to same-sex partners. The gay and lesbian movement screamed bloody murder and sued, and the Colorado State Supreme Court overruled the will of the people. The same thing is happening in California. As I write this part of the book, that state's Supreme Court has just decided to overturn Proposition 8 (which outlawed same-sex marriages), as approved by the voters, and decided it was discriminatory. Well I am sorry, but if the voters say it will be this way or that way, that should be the end of it, as set forth by our Founding Fathers. However, today's world feels that if one person is offended or denied an action, or something like that, then the voters must be overruled. Bull! I don't like having President Barack Obama as my president, but that was the will of the people.

On this issue, we have no common sense, or even common ground, in our country compared to what is in our Constitution. The way our president, Congress, and courts are acting, you would not know that we even have a constitution. When our Founding Fathers decided to empower the people with the final say in the decisions of our nation, they simply used common sense in letting the majority rule. Sure, there have been things we did not like being approved, but at least we had our say in it. But what good is having our say when the courts, our president, and Congress have no desire to follow the will of the people?

Issue 2—Abortion

In my opinion, there is no more divisive issue in our country than that of abortion. You do not have to be on the staff of a major university medical center, hospital, or the like to determine that life begins at conception. Every person who has lived, is alive today, or will live in the future started out as an egg being fertilized by a sperm inside of their mother's womb. To say that life does not exist until birth is simply nuts, shows narrow-minded thinking, and makes no sense at all.

The 1973 Roe vs. Wade ruling by the Supreme Court showed a plain disregard for life, and not a single one of the judges on that court should be proud of that ruling. Talk about the lack of common sense. How did those justices think they became a person, and who gave them the right to determine if a life can be terminated? There are so many medical facts to prove that life begins at conception, yet we still have doctors supporting the right to abortion. This is one of those issues where there are two sides to the issue. One is right and the other is wrong, and abortion is wrong. In fact, it is murder in the purest sense of the word.

Even common sense allows for three exceptions on this issue. If the mother's life is in danger by continuing the pregnancy, it only makes sense to terminate. Otherwise you might lose both the baby and the mother. The other two are debatable, and I know some who disagree with me on this opinion completely, both Christian and non-Christian. If a woman of any age becomes pregnant as the result of a rape or incest, I feel she has the right to ask for the baby to be aborted. First, she must have reported the rape or act of incest to the appropriate authorities and aided in the prosecution of the violator. Then, and only then, should she be given the option to have the abortion. I do not believe God would disapprove of any of these three options, because the use of one's clear thinking, simple understanding, and knowledge of the facts and long-term effects apply to the need of the woman involved.

The case of a mother's life being in danger is easy to understand and should not need any further explanation. However, the woman who is a victim of rape or of incest can be affected for life. It is bad enough that it happened at all, but then to require her to carry the baby to term, deal with the ridicule from her peers, go through the delivery, and raise the child could cause long-term difficulties for the woman, and the child. (Of course, adoption is always a possibility on this issue and should not be ignored in the mother making her decision.) The issue will never go away. The child would be the product of a crime, and both the mother and the child would have to live with that for life. So the use of common sense in determining whether the woman will or will not get the abortion is needed, but ultimately the decision must come from the woman and only her.

On this issue, our courts have again interfered with the will of the people, or in this case, those who the people elected to Congress and the presidency. During President George W. Bush's first term in office, the Congress voted by large margins in both the House of Representatives and the Senate to send the partial-birth abortion bill to the president. He signed it into law in November of 2003, just as he had promised during his speech at the Republican National Convention where he was nominated as their candidate in 2000.

Just a short time later, a woman felt her civil rights to an abortion were being denied by this law, and she brought a suit before a federal judge in Nebraska. He ruled her rights were being denied, and his ruling declared the new law as unconstitutional. Who did this judge think he was, overruling Congress and the president, the final word in the country? Even Senator Dianne Feinstein (D-California), who voted against the law, said that the Congress established the law, the president signed it into law, and no one judge should be able to overrule it just because one person did not like the law. In 2007, the United States Supreme Court ruled that the law was constitutional, based on the case of Gonzalez vs. Carhart.

Because there is such a lack of common sense in our country, we just do not stop to think what we are doing, what the adverse affects might be, and who they might affect or hurt in the long run of things in life. God may, or may not, approve of the three exceptions I explained above, but I can guarantee you that He does not like this country letting women get abortions on demand. If a woman goes to a party, out for a good time, or whatever the situation, and gets pregnant from it, well, you have made your bed, honey. Play with things like pregnancy and you might just get bitten by them. On this part of the abortion issue, a woman getting an abortion is just plain murder and should not be allowed in our country. When you use no common sense when dating or partying, you have to pay the price!

Issue 3—Public Display of Religious Articles

Nothing steams me more than when one person gets upset about a nativity scene at Christmas or a cross on a church or gravesites or takes it upon him or herself to sue anyone who tries to display such items in public. In recent years, we have had efforts to eliminate the word *Christmas* from our very vocabulary as a nation, preventing employees from saying "Merry Christmas" to customers for fear of being sued by the American Civil Liberties Union (ACLU) or the Americans United for the Separation of Church and State (AUSCS). A cross that has existed in the Mohave Desert since the 1930's is all of a sudden an offense to someone, so it was stolen, and on it goes.

These are simply attempts to remove God from our country. They do not offend anyone, they do not hurt anyone, and if you do not like it, just look away. Instead, we who do like these displays are denied our freedom of expression provided for in the First Amendment to the Constitution. But the issue here is that these protests are against items that are associated with Christianity only. Put up a red crescent in honor of Islam, something to do with the worship of Buddha, or any other religion and you will not hear a thing being said or done. In fact, recently the news reported that some are even upset about the crosses that mark our World War II dead in Normandy, France. Talk about a lack of common sense. This is just plain being hateful and ridiculous.

Again the courts have created this situation by making stupid rulings. The Supreme Court even ruled that burning the American flag in public was protected under the freedom of expression. What a pound of cow manure! Thank goodness Congress stepped in on this one and overruled that decision. I fly my American flag in front of my home, and this past Fourth of July, my wife even placed rubber magnets on our garage door saying, "God Bless America." If anyone had tried to remove any of them, he or she would have known that I was not happy.

If it were not for the grace of God Almighty and His mercy to us as a country, I truly believe we would have been conquered long ago. When we have to change calling a Christmas tree to calling it a holiday tree or Christmas to winter holiday, these are simply attempts to remove the word *Christ* from our country. The word *Christmas* itself originated from the combining of two words, *Christ* and *mass* (as in a Catholic service). If you do not want to honor God and believe in Jesus Christ and that He died for your sins on that cruel Roman cross, that is your decision. I believe you will pay for rejecting Him in the afterlife, but that is my belief. However, in the same manner, do not deny my right to believe in Jesus Christ and publicly display that belief.

If hearing the Bible being read, anything about God, hearing the name Jesus Christ, seeing a cross, seeing a nativity scene, or someone wishing you "Merry Christmas" makes you nervous, maybe you should find out why. You can deny God all day and every day, but that does not make God not exist. Just because you do not want to be wished "Merry Christmas" does not mean the person behind you does not want to. Get this straight: all you need to do is look around you at the birds, trees, sun, moon, and stars to know God does exist. Common sense will tell you that this world did not come from a big bang, and we did not come from a little one-celled animal. This is what we will deal with in the next issue.

Issue 4—Evolution vs. Intelligent Design (Creation)

In our schools and during school board meetings, the issue of teaching evolution and/or creation (today called Intelligent Design) brings out more contention between the two parties than any other education issue I know. In this chapter on dividing issues, this one is probably the most divisive of them all at Parent Teacher Organization (PTO) meetings or in relation to our school administrators and principals. There is no common ground on this issue either. You either believe in evolution and not in God or in creation or believe in God.

On the many issues, and other chapters of this book, this one will be the hardest for me to be fair on, as I am a firm believer in God's existence and that He created all that is in the universe. However, I will attempt to be fair by asking several questions to you, as if we were having a debate on this issue. I will ask the question and then give you my reason for believing God created all and that it did not just happen.

Question 1: Explain the big bang thing to me. How did it create the universe?

It is my understanding that there are two theories of thinking on this occurrence. One is that a large star went supernova and blew up, and all that we know today was made from the fragments of the star that flew outward from it, putting in place the sun, the moon and stars, and the rest of the universe. The second one is that two large objects crashed into each other, causing the big bang, and all that we know today was put into place.

If you want evolution taught in our schools as fact, I think you better come to some kind of agreement on how it happened to start with and then present your argument for it being fact. To me, this just proves it is nothing but a theory, and a bad one at that, so on this answer you cannot be right. Further, this makes it clear that you cannot teach evolution as a fact. You need to explain where the large star or the two objects came from to start with to even cause the big bang. Except for God (and I am speaking of the Trinity of God the Father, God the Son, and God the Holy Spirit), everything has a beginning, so where did these things come from? Who created them?

Question 2: What naturally occurring chemical reaction happened to start life on earth, and why only here and no other place that we have been able to confirm?

I do not claim to be a biologist, biochemist, biotech engineer, or anything like that; but from what I know, the chemical makeup of a single-celled animal like the amoeba has no relation to the human cell makeup or DNA. In fact, I know of no creature that exists like the amoeba. If so, would you please introduce me to a two-celled animal, a four-celled animal, etc.?

If all life came from a single-celled animal, how did it come into existence? What chemical reaction caused it to come to life? Why, if we all came from this same source, do we have so many different species of animals? Where is the missing link between the chimpanzee and humans?

Today we have dogs, cats, horses, cattle, llamas, koala bears, snakes, lions, tigers, and every insect you can imagine here on earth. And you are going to tell me that all came from the same single-celled source? If the universe came into existence as you say, why don't these types of creatures exist on other planets, and why do these other planets have differing types of atmospheres or none at all?

This part of the evolution theory (and I will not call it anything else) has so many holes in it, it makes Swiss cheese look like a solid block. On top of the several questions I have laid out as my argument against evolution, for this question segment, you would also have to explain why humans are warm-blooded creations and animals like snakes are cold blooded. It is easy to say that this is the way is happened, but it is much harder to prove it, especially when you cannot do so.

Question 3: Where did the trees and plants come from, and how did they start?

Ask any botanist, professional gardener, or forestry expert, and they will tell you that all plants are alive. Plant life on earth is also part of life here on earth, and somewhere down the line evolutionists forgot to explain where they came from or how they started after the big bang.

Unlike humans, and other animals like my guide dog Jodi, plants breathe carbon dioxide. God set up this perfect exchange of atmospheres, the air we breathe versus what the plants breathe, to cause a continual regeneration of our air and their air. If all life came from that single-celled animal, how is it that some breathe our oxygen/nitrogen atmosphere and others breathe the carbon dioxide atmosphere on the same planet? If life exists on other planets, how do they breathe the poisonous atmosphere of Venus (or so the scientists tell us), or how do they exist on planets with no atmosphere, like Mercury?

Question 4: Explain to me why the skeleton of Cro-Magnon man in the Smithsonian's Natural History Museum looks so much like a gorilla's skeleton.

Wait, I thought you said we are descendants of the chimpanzee? Chimps and gorillas do not look alike or act alike and are not even the same size. Are we trying to insert a fifth ace into this deck of cards? Are you saying that we originally went from a single-celled animal, through all of the small steps of evolving into looking like the gorilla first, and then we looked like the chimps? Boy do you have a lot of explaining to do on this one. Do you realize how many different kinds of monkeys exist on earth? Okay, so narrow this down for me. Which one did we really come from, and please take all of the time you need to prove it?

Question 5: We have animals and trees on land, so where did the birds come from, and who taught them to fly?

Again, you are telling us we came from a single-celled animal. So what happened to make some of the evolutionary creatures of today fly? How did they develop feathers and so many types? Stumped on this one? I know the answer! God said so, and it happened.

Question 6: Where did the dinosaurs go?

Let me be direct on this question. I do believe that dinosaurs existed on this earth at one time. So where are they now? All you have are the bones, and yes that is proof that they did exist, but where are they now? Ever hear about something called Noah and the flood in chapter 6 of Genesis in the Bible?

Under this question I also have to ask how you know they existed over one hundred million years ago and more in some cases. Carbon-14 testing has been proven to be faulty more often than it is accurate. Further, any qualified coroner, forensics expert, or medical examiner will tell you that after a long period of exposure to the ground, bones will also break down into dust. Yeah I know, the dinosaurs are supposed to have been petrified, preserving their bones for millions of years. Well I am not buying that one, based on what the experts say about how the earth breaks down body parts after long exposure.

Recently, charges were put forth that one of our founding fathers, former President Thomas Jefferson, fathered a child with one of his African American slave girls. The descendants of this slave girl got a court to rule that President Jefferson's body could be exhumed for DNA testing. When they opened the grave, which was located on the Monticello estate in Virginia, they did not find much. There were a few bone fragments and mostly dirt. The wooden casket and a majority of the body had broken down into the dust of the earth. He died in 1826, and his bones were all but gone already. What makes you think that the dinosaur's bones could last for millions of years without the same results?

Question 7: What is so difficult about believing in God and that He created everything on earth and in the heavens?

You college-educated folks always think something has to be complicated and take a lot of analysis before it can be accepted as fact. You are so convinced that evolution is true and feel it should be taught in our schools as fact, but you cannot prove it to save yourselves. In fact, you cannot prove that you even exist.

The problem is that you just cannot allow yourself to believe that there is a supreme being, God, who simply said it and all was created as we know it today (read about the six days of creation in Genesis chapters 1 and 2). I only dealt with the animals on the land, the birds in the air, and the plants on earth. What about all the different species of fish, shelled animals, crabs, and jellyfish that make up our oceans, rivers, and streams? How come some live in salt water and others in fresh water? It could go on and on, and all you will do is look at me and not know what to say.

Evolution is not a fact; it is a theory just to be able to deny the existence of God. It is your out from having to live under God's directions for your life. In the questions I asked, I have completely unraveled this theory. It does not belong in our schools. If your school board will not remove it, then get elected to the board and remove it yourself.

All you need to do is look around and list the different types of plants you see, birds in the air, and animals at the local zoo. Somewhere down the line you have to believe that all of these different kinds of living things could not have come from just a single-celled chemical occurrence. It just does not make any sense, common sense in this case.

Issue 5—Showing Love to Your Neighbors, Even if They Disagree with You

We have dealt with several issues, but certainly not all, that can and do cause us to create differences between each other in today's world. The fact that we are all different is what makes each and every one of us unique, and it is these differences that lead to great ideas and inventions and a better life for all of us. But if we allow them to cause a rift between us just because we want our way, and only our way, then that is what we will get, and nothing will be resolved.

I know a fellow Christian who vehemently disagrees with me that dinosaurs existed. He believes the bones in the Smithsonian are nothing but papier-mâché creations, just to make people believe in the creatures. We stand in disagreement on this, but that does not make him or me any less of a Christian or a person in each other's eyes. First, find common ground with each other. If a certain issue is divisive, avoid it if all possible, but do not compromise your faith in what you believe. In my case, he can disagree with me all he wants, but I still believe dinosaurs did exist. It is those issues that make no sense at all, like evolution being taught in our schools as fact, where we need to draw the line in the sand.

In my years of learning how to be a Christian, I have learned that arguing with a fool is completely senseless. If people do not want to believe in God, that is their decision, and all I can do is pray that somewhere down the line they will see the truth in what I said. Further, I pray that they will see it before it is too late. The day that

God will have had His fill of this evil and sinful world is coming. Are you ready?

The best example of how to do this comes from when Jesus walked this earth. He was known all around for His compassion for the people. He healed the sick and showed love to those who even hated Him. However, one day when Jesus walked into the temple area, He found the money changers doing their business, took out a whip, and chased them away from His Father's house (John 2:13–16 NIV). He drew the line with those people and made a stand for what was right. We should use this example when differences come up between us and those around us. Remember, everybody is our neighbor, not just those who live next door or across the street.

To my fellow Christians reading this book, this does not mean we have to just step back and say nothing on an issue. Many Christians have let known their outrage about evolution in our schools, and Intelligent Design is not allowed to be mentioned. Let your voice be heard. It is a right under our Constitution, and if that does not work, see you at the voting booth.

Chapter 4

See You in Court

The use of common sense in our courtrooms today is lacking so much, you would think it was a disease that all involved try to avoid. From the rulings coming down by judges to decisions by juries to the very reasons the hearings are even being held, you would swear (a little courtroom humor there) that common sense had been replaced by idiocracy. In my previous chapters, and in my book *Time Witnessing*, I addressed some of the rulings by federal judges, but other rulings should also be discussed, and will in this chapter. In past decisions by jurors, it makes you wonder which case they were listening to, because their decisions made no sense at all. Then there are the many reasons for people filing court actions. People are suing each other and companies for, in their opinion, denying them their civil rights, and most of these actions are frivolous, to put it mildly.

I was always taught that judges are in place to enforce the laws of our land, oversee cases in accordance with the rule of law, and make their decision based on the law as it exists at that time. However, in today's decisions, our judges are actually making law or taking it upon themselves to overrule the lawmakers in our state and federal legislatures.

In 1954, Congress added the words, "One nation, under God…" to the Pledge of Allegiance. In 2002, the California ninth Circuit Court of Appeals ruled by a two-to-one margin that these words were unconstitutional. This ruling was the result of a suit filed by an atheist father who did not want his daughter to be required to say these words.

First, where did this court get the idea that they could overrule Congress? They are the lawmakers, and we are "one nation," as in the United States, and our Founding Fathers established our country "under God." You can find this fact in the Declaration of Independence, the preamble to the Constitution, on our money, and even engraved on some of our federal buildings in Washington DC. Second, Congress is required by the Constitution to uphold that document in its making of law and passing of legislation. If, in 1954, the Congress and then-President Dwight Eisenhower did not think that these words violated the Constitution, why did this court feel it did in 2002? Simple common sense on the part of that court should have told them to throw this suit out from the start.

Adding to this problem, the Supreme Court overruled the appeals court, but not because it was totally ridiculous and frivolous. They overruled that court because of procedural discrepancies. What a cowardly sidestep that was, as they should have simply stated that the reason for the suit was unfounded and baseless. Darn, our Supreme Court justices cannot spell common sense either!

Another thing judges are doing today is throwing out cases because the defendants are claiming abuse by police, that they were not read their Miranda rights soon enough, or some other kind of crybaby claims. If criminals see that by making these stupid claims they can get their cases dismissed, they will shout these claims right from the start. It does not matter that they are resisting arrest, punching out the police officers making the arrest, or anything like that.

I know if I were a judge, these criminals would be scared to death to come before me. I would use the Judge Roy Beam method of running my courtroom. You did what? Take him out back and shoot him. Next case! Now that may be a bit humorous, but I really do believe that if the old time Western-type justice was utilized with these criminals today, crime would go way down.

As a side note, today's criminals are being sentenced to prisons that are more like resorts than correctional facilities. They have televisions, computer access, libraries, and recreational yards for their use. We the taxpayers provide for their medical care, food, and clothing and pay for the buildings to house them. I know, I have heard the stories of brutality in the prisons, but for the most part, what a life. No bills, everything is provided to you, and if the air conditioning goes out, pity the managers of that facility in the eyes of Amnesty International. I have firsthand knowledge of this, as my brother-in-law is a guard at a prison in Pennsylvania.

As a final whack on the judges, I am still steamed about the judge in Florida who ruled that a lady in a vegetative state (the result of a heart-related medical problem) would be allowed to starve to death by removing her feeding tube. What? Where was the preservation of life on this one? She was not on life support. She was in a state that I am not qualified to explain, but the only care she needed was being fed by a tube into her stomach. She could have been kept in a nursing care facility.

Her husband, who by this time had fathered a child with another woman, needed to find a way out of the marriage, and the woman was not in a state to understand anything to sign off on a divorce decree. So he pursued action by the court to order her feeding tube removed. After several months of back and forth on this, the judge ruled that the tube could be removed, and the lady was allowed to simply starve to death and died. Make your own decision on this one, but I call this murder.

In today's world, I think one of the hardest civic duties to perform is that of an impartial juror, especially when you end up, if chosen, on a jury deciding a civil case between people, families, or a person and a corporation. These civil cases are so full of perjurous lies of he said/she said that determining who is right and who is wrong is challenging to say the least. Then you have the lawyers who take these cases for the publicity and of course the money. Add to this the types of judges today, as described before, and what a problem for the juror.

Despite these situations, some of the decisions from juries in the past years have been nothing short of biased, racial, or in some cases plain stupid. They are biased because of who is being accused of what, racial because of who is involved (plaintiffs and/or defendants), and stupid because you wonder if the same jury that sat through the court case was the same one to make the decision in the case.

I know that some doctors today are plainly inept and frankly should not be in the profession. There is a doctor in our area who is so well known for being a quack that the local hospital will not allow him in the facility. Another one serves a local nursing care facility not because he is good but because he is cheap. Good he isn't, and the nurses (my wife is one of them) in that facility will tell you so too. However, there are other doctors who are being sued today just because someone's loved one did not survive a surgery, they feel not enough was done to fight off the cancer, or the doctor did not do enough to help them. So they take them to court, suing them for malpractice.

During the case, the family members will get on the stand, cry a lot, and try to tell their story how they feel the doctor failed them and their family member who died. Then the doctor's lawyers will present all of the tests ordered by the physician, the efforts made to correct the medical situation, details of any surgical procedures, and medicines prescribed in an attempt to show that all that could be done was done.

While the doctor's lawyers cross-examine the experts, and especially the family members, they usually end up facing blubbering idiots. The experts usually have no idea about the details of the person's history but just talk about what other tests could have been ordered or why the doctor misinterpreted the test results. In cross-examining the doctor and his witnesses, the plaintiff's lawyers will put on a show for the jury of how the doctor took away the family member by failing to do what was necessary, even if not possible, just to plant the seed of guilt.

In today's medical world, the primary care physicians do not usually interpret test results. These results come from specialists in that area of medicine, for example: x-rays, blood tests, etc. From that information, the doctor makes a determination of the medical care, prescriptions, or treatments that will aid the person in getting better. In the case of those who are diagnosed with something terminal, cancer and the like, doctors do what can be done to comfort the person until the inevitable time of his or her death arrives.

If the jury utilizes common sense, they will get expert information on the situation, review the arguments, and from that make a decision in the case. Unfortunately, pity for the family, or just plain bias for the surviving members, rules the day. The doctor is found guilty of malpractice, and the family is awarded big bucks as compensation. This is why the cost of medical care is rising in our country today, so the doctors can protect themselves from these biased decisions and pay for the insurance.

I may be stepping on sacred ground on this issue, but I cannot remember a more obvious case of racial bias than that of the jury decision in the murder case against O. J. Simpson. But the jury members were not the only individuals showing either bias or plain ineptness in this case. First, Judge Lance Ito looked like he was asleep during some of the televised case or was certainly not paying attention to the proceedings. The obvious stunts by the defense team were nothing short of stupid and created a circus atmosphere within the courtroom. Judge Ito should have sustained, instead of overruling, the prosecution's objection to having O. J. try on the bloody glove. Anyone with an ounce of common sense would have known that the glove would have shrunk in size from the soaking of the blood on it. But no, he allowed that circus stunt, and the jury bought it. Okay, enough said, but you get my point.

Then there are the plain stupid decisions by juries. One cost a popular burger chain an undisclosed amount of compensation, and in the other cases, cost the tobacco industry billions eventually. In these cases I will write about below, the companies were punished for the person's plain idiocracy and stupidity.

In the first case (Liebeck vs. McDonald's) in 1994, a lady ordered a cup of coffee from the burger chain's drive-up window. After receiving it from the employee, she placed it in an unsecure manner in the car, paid the worker, and drove off. In doing so, the cup spilled onto her and burned her. Instead of blaming herself for a stupid move, she chose to sue the burger chain for failing to tell her that the coffee was hot.

In the case, the lawyers for the burger chain argued that common sense would tell a person that the coffee was hot. After all, they do not sell cold coffee! Second, the cup should have been placed into a cup holder and not where it was not supported securely. That makes perfectly good sense to me, but not so to the jury. They found the burger chain negligent in warning the person that the coffee was hot and awarded her over two million dollars. Eventually, an out-of-court settlement was reached between the parties for an undisclosed amount. There is no way to be fair on this one. That lady was stupid, blamed her ineptness on a totally innocent source, and got big bucks out of it. If I had been the CEO of that company, I would have appealed that lady into bankruptcy from lawyer fees. This decision is below stupid. It just does not make any common sense at all.

In the many cases against the tobacco industry, people who were dying from cancer caused by years of smoking sued the tobacco industry for causing their cancer. Let me be fair here. Smoking does cause cancer, and every pack has a warning on it that tells the purchaser of this possibility since the surgeon general ordered it added to cigarette packs in 1965. Even NASCAR stopped calling its highest class of competition the Winston Cup, which refers to the brand of cigarettes.

Despite these facts, many suits have been filed in court. The tobacco industry lawyers have argued to no avail of the warnings placed on every pack and that nobody forced the people to buy the first pack of cigarettes, nor any packs after that first one. Among the idiotic claims that some people have stated in these cases are that their name was not on the warning label. Here is a prime example where people failed to, or did not know to, read the warning and the industry had to pay out the nose for their stupidity. In the late 1990's, a settlement between the tobacco industry and the federal government led to the industry paying over two hundred billion dollars to the states for medical-related compensation.

We have yet to deal with the basis of these idiotic decisions by judges and juries. That is, of course, why the suits were filed in the first place within our courts. Somebody does not like what somebody else did or feels they took their song or invention. Neighbors are suing neighbors, organizations are suing organizations, and on it goes in America. The biggest problem in this area is a total lack of common sense. People, groups, and organizations are not stopping to think and consider the ramifications and ill effects their actions will cause in this country. Neither are they taking into account the time they are taking away from the courts to deal with more valid cases. No, instead they want their way, only their way, and without it, they file a suit.

What is amazing about some of these suits is that they involve Christian symbols. I am convinced that those who do not want to acknowledge there is a God do not want or feel that they need to answer to a supreme being or must prove to themselves (as well as others too) that there is no God. They are the reason behind these frivolous suits.

Finally, it is time for our Congress to weigh in on these judges who are overruling and declaring that laws are un constitutional just because one or more individuals feel their civil rights have been denied. As I stated before, the Congress and the president have sworn, at the time of their election and taking office, that they will uphold the Constitution. So where do the judges come from when they declare a law is unconstitutional that the other two components of our government have put into place as constitutional . Also, Congress needs to make it very clear that when the voters decide an issue in one way or the other, that is final. If it takes a constitutional amendment, so be it, but these actions that overrule the people have got to stop. What is next? Will people sue because they were not elected president, and by declaring that their right to serve in that position was denied, will the court put them in office instead of the elected person?

Chapter 5

Getting Rid of Christ in Our Country

Read in the Bible: Isaiah 26:12–14, Ezekiel 36:19–21 (NIV).

There are two phrases commonly used as cursing that I do not tolerate in my presence. You do not say God damn or Jesus Christ when speaking to me. I am offended and consider it the defaming of my God and Savior. However, for the most part, my wishes to not hear these curse words are just ignored or flipped off by others. They take the attitude that if I do not like it, too bad. Even if I wanted to, I would get nowhere in a court of law suing about these words being used in my presence, because the court would simply rule that the person was exercising his or her freedom of speech and expression. In fact, at the time of this writing, the ACLU has just won a case where a person was charged and fined for use of profanity toward a police officer and another person involved in the incident. But when it comes to removing Christ from our country, the courts seem to be willing to listen and rule in favor of the plaintiff in these cases.

I dealt earlier, and in my book *Time Witnessing*, with the ninth Circuit Court's ruling on the phrase "One nation, under God…" from our Pledge of Allegiance. But many other court actions have been filed or threatened that would remove references to God, Jesus Christ, or anything associated with Christianity from our society. Just a few years ago, the Social Progressives (SP's), or far lefters, decided that saying "Merry Christmas" was offensive to the public and threatened to sue retailers who allowed their employees to say this phrase. After a nationwide uprising about this and threatened boycotts of the retailers, the employees were again allowed to say "Merry Christmas," and in one case were even encouraged to do so. This is one case where the public (the majority of people) overruled the SP's, a very small minority of the people. They simply hit the retailers where it would hurt them worst, right in their sales bottom line. They said if you do not allow the employees to say "Merry Christmas," we will take our dollars to someone who will, and it worked. But the SP folks still do not get the message. Efforts are still continuing in an attempt to get Christmas changed to winter holiday. But where is the common sense in these efforts? By doing this, Bing Crosby's famous song "White Christmas" will have to be re-recorded as white winter holiday. The song "It Is Beginning to Look A Lot like Christmas" would have to be changed to winter holiday. This is just nuts.

Let me sound off at this point. These SP folks like to think they are progressive thinkers, but the truth is that they should be called social regressives, because their actions are causing our country to regress into a socialist/atheistic lifestyle.

Then you have the school administrators across the country who are so afraid of offending and subsequently being sued by someone that they will not allow any references to God in school plays or at graduation ceremonies. A school in the state of Washington was not allowed to present the Charles Dickens play "A Christmas Carol" because the character Tiny Tim said at one place, "God bless us all" in the script. (I guess the SP folks would like to change the title of this play to a winter holiday carol too.) However, if Tiny Tim would say, "May Allah bless us all," that would be all right? Or how about, "May Buddha bless us all"? This is not just without common sense; it is just plain stupid. The issue is to remove Christ from our hearing and society.

Also being attacked today is the public display of the Ten Commandments or a cross. Again, this is simply another attempt to remove God and Christianity from our society. In one case, the removal of the public display of the Ten Commandments cost the Chief Justice of the Alabama Supreme Court, Judge Roy Moore, his position on that court. What are the SP's, ACLU, AUSCS, and the atheists afraid of when they see these symbols? I know the answer: the truth that God does exist and is in control of this world. They think by removing any references to God, Jesus Christ, and Christmas, people will not think about anything other than what they want them to think and know about in this country.

Talk about your lack of common sense and not knowing how to spell it. These organizations must think we are a bunch of zombies walking around this nation. Well word up, you folks, we are not zombies, but you are totally nuts if you think we are going to just sit back and let you take God out of our nation. From the time of the Pilgrims to today, this nation has been founded on our belief in God, and that is just the way it is going to stay.

I want to deal with this issue of removing crosses from the public eye, and in addition, I want to take issue with you folks who pitch a fit about cities across this nation putting up nativity scenes at Christmas. The bottom line here is your desperate need to do all you can to deny that Jesus Christ even existed, lived in what is referred to as the Holy Land today (or Israel), died on a Roman cross, and rose again to conquer death. No matter how much history confirms that these events actually occurred, you just cannot have it this way. Well too bad! These events are just as much fact as creation itself and are able to be proven just as much. The very fact that you do all that can be done, in total desperation, to remove God from our schools and public buildings is evidence enough of the fact that it is true. Why else would you try so hard and do all that you can to convince the courts to remove this evidence?

The even bigger issue is that there is not a single drop of common sense in your efforts to remove Christianity from the United States.

I go back to a previous statement that it must be your way and only your way on this issue of no crosses and no public prayers at games or special events. Anything that refers to Christ in any way must go. This is just plain stupid and shows a great lack of maturity on your part.

Now you probably are screaming, "Where is your fairness all of a sudden in this book?" It is still here, but you need to see why it is senseless to butt up against the very foundations of our country. I would be the first person to defend your right to assemble against what you do not like, express your dislike of it, and put forth your best argument against the issue. It is your constitutional right to do so but not to do it at another person's expense.

This is a democracy, where the majority rules. In Congress, some bills, resolutions, or measures require only a simple majority of the members present (if a quorum exists) to approve the legislation. Others require a two-thirds vote to pass the measure, like an amendment to the Constitution. However, in accordance with the Constitution, we the voters of this nation each have one vote (once you are eighteen years of age). When a vote is taken, it is supposed to be final. So if the majority votes to deny same-sex marriages, like in California's Proposition 8, that is the way it is. But no, because you did not get your way, you run to the courts, and then they overrule the voters. I close this chapter with a question. So what is next, outlawing the singing of Christmas carols in public?

Chapter 6

Using the Military to Defend Our Borders

Up until the time of President Harry S. Truman, the Cabinet post that oversees our military was called the War Department. However, after World War II, the name was changed to the Department of Defense (DOD). It was also at this time in our nation's history that the great seal of the United States was changed to show the eagle's head looking at the olive branch instead of the arrows, in an effort to show we prefer peace over war.

The Revolutionary War was fought for our independence from England, and for freedom. The War of 1812 was fought to keep those freedoms. We fought each other in the Civil War, just because some idiots wanted to make some humans remain as slaves. (Not our greatest hour!) The Spanish/American War, World War I, and World War II were fought in response to an attack on our nation in one way or another.

Then we fought wars in Korea, Vietnam, and most recently the two wars in Iraq (Desert Storm and Operation Iraqi Freedom) as well as the war in Afghanistan. These wars were fought to help another country keep from falling into communism, in the case of Korea and Vietnam; to free an invaded nation in Kuwait; and then to deal with a tyrant who probably had something to do with the 9/11 attacks in Operation Iraqi Freedom (OIF).

Sending our nation's young men and women to war in response to an attack on us or to help defend a country from communism is one thing, but we are not the world's police and defenders. I know that there is a fine line here, and I cannot say I am firmly on one side or the other. What one person considers a valid reason to send in our troops another person may be in total disagreement about. Because of this, I feel that this is where we need to trust our leaders, but we also need to get on our knees and pray for them.

The responsibility of the presidency, as commander in chief of our armed forces, is a very humbling and difficult one to say the least. I have great respect for those difficult decisions made by past presidents. Three of them stand out to me more than any others. First, then-President Harry S. Truman knew that we could not take much more of World War II, so he ordered the atom bomb dropped on two Japanese cities. It was a dangerous decision, but history shows that it was the right one. The second one was President Ronald Reagan. Without firing a shot, he built up our country's military, proposed the Star Wars anti-missile system, and took down the Soviet Union.

Although I could cite many past decisions by our presidents, I chose these two examples because they showed the nation what they (the presidents) were made of and that when a decision had to be made, they made them. It took guts, wisdom, good intelligence, and above all, common sense. President Truman had to choose between two bombs and the possible loss of up to another two hundred fifty thousand or more soldiers in invading Japan. President Reagan's actions and decisions put then-Soviet leader Mikhail Gorbachev in a position that gave him no wiggle room when meeting in Iceland.

However, by far the best show of guts, wisdom, and common sense was that of President John F. Kennedy, during the Cuban Missile Crisis. History shows us now, but few knew then, how close we came to nuclear war with the Union of Soviet Socialist Republics (USSR). The then-leader of the USSR, Nikita Khrushchev, was determined to put us in a place of all but surrendering to their desire to rule the world. President Kennedy simply made it clear that if he wanted war, he was going to get it. Every long range missile we had was placed on alert, targets were established, and Nikita blinked. To put it plainly, President Kennedy plain out stared Nikita down.

In the case of President Truman's decision, he saw the grim future of continuing the war on the ground, and using the bombs offensively, he actually saved many many more lives on both sides. President Kennedy saved the world from total destruction, and it brought Nikita down eventually. Finally, President Reagan just simply used common sense, put the military in a good place to defend our interests and security, made the USSR's missiles useless, and down came communism and the Soviet Union. These three presidents used their military to defend the United States, and that is what it should be used for in every case. We are not the world's police, and we do not have all the answers, so we need to get our noses out of where they do not belong.

It is not necessarily the best thing to take the war to the enemy, like in the case of our war with the Taliban in Afghanistan. Instead, we need to put our forces in a position where we can do the most damage and make the enemy run for the hills. In the case of Afghanistan, we need to simply bomb the mountains where the Taliban are hiding and maybe add a little napalm and burn them up. Maybe we should put some of those smart bombs to work on the caves. Remember, I said that the military Cabinet post is now the Department of Defense. That is just what we should use our soldiers for too. I do not disagree that we need a Department of Homeland Security (DHS), but it cannot handle all of the border issues. The military should be charged with doing just what it is, the defense of our nation. The Coast Guard can guard the coast, but they cannot do a thing with our border with Mexico and the drug and immigration problem. Here is where our military can help secure these land borders and stop the border crossings and illegal aliens issue.

I cannot believe how naive our current president and his administration are to the illegal crossings going on in our country's southwestern area. The border between the United States and Mexico is over two thousand miles long, and we only have enough border guards to handle one man for every ten or more miles. Even with the unmanned drones, cameras, and what fencing there is, that just will not cut it, folks. Common sense would tell you to use the defense of our nation, but *no*, we cannot do this, believe it or not, by law.

Did you know that there is a law in our country that states that the military cannot be used for law enforcement? Yep, Congress strikes again! Someone in their infinite wisdom (idiocracy in my opinion), clear back in the mid-1800's, felt that the military should not be involved in this part of our country's security, and the law was put in place. Well, this is just plain nuts, and common sense was definitely on vacation during that time. Who better to shut down those borders, enforce our immigration laws, and prevent the drug trade from invading our nation? If they are the defense of our nation, then let's use them for our defense against the drug dealers, runners, and illegals. I am pretty sure I know what the reason may have been for this law, but if the military wanted to do something in this country, no law would prevent it from happening.

I will be the first person to defend a person wanting to legally immigrate into our country, but notice I wrote legally. If you get a visa to enter and then decide to become naturalized, welcome aboard. Except for the Native Americans (Navaho, Cherokee, Apache, etc.), all of us are immigrants to this country. In my case, my descendants came from Germany and settled in the area of Altoona, Pennsylvania. But entering illegally is not the way to come into the United States, and we need to stop this wave of people at the borders.

Common sense would tell you that if you are going to pay for a trained and strong military, then let them do what they do best: defend our borders. When put up against our military forces, the Mexican drug cartels would be no match. I really feel that if we utilized the armed forces of our country to lock down the borders, the crime rate in the whole nation would drop dramatically. Also, the military would continue to be subordinate to the civilian leadership. In no way am I suggesting or endorsing a bigger place in our government for the military. I just feel that common sense would tell you to use the DOD for our defense against this type of criminal element.

Chapter 7

Private vs. Public Health Care

In May of 2010, President Barack Obama got his beloved health care bill. The bill that was in excess of two thousand five hundred pages, brought in a whole new litany of regulations and insurance company requirements, and blew the top off of our nation's deficit. The bill that is loaded with hidden changes, regulations, etc., is made up of a little bit of wording the common person could understand and quite a bit of lawyer lingo that just does not need to be in the bill. However, what is not in the bill is the desire of the SP folks to eventually move us into a public health care system, like that in Canada, Great Britain, and other countries. This idea is already being discussed across our land, and we need to give it fair hearing in this book.

In my job, I have worked with people who live in Canada and Great Britain. In talking with them, the reactions are quite mixed on their opinions of a public health care system. My friend in Canada thinks it is great and tells me that she has never had a problem getting to see a doctor or obtaining emergency health assistance. Also, my wife and I spoke to a couple from Canada while on vacation, and they repeated the same feelings. However, some of those I have spoken to in Great Britain have had just the opposite experiences. Now whether it is run better in Canada than in Great Britain, I cannot say, nor can they, but it is probably just like anything else in this world. It has its good parts and its bad parts.

If we look at the current health care we have here in the United States, we could say the same things. I recently had a situation where I had to go to my local emergency room, and I ended up waiting six and one-half hours before I had the problem resolved. It took all that time and a bill to my insurance company in excess of one thousand dollars, and most of the time I just laid in the bed waiting on the doctor to come and help me.

In this case, the only difference between our system and that of Canada and Great Britain was that I left with a bill in hand; they don't. Another issue between the systems is the claim that the public system may make you wait several months to see a specialist or even a primary care physician. My local orthopedic surgeon has quite a schedule, and if I called today for an appointment, it would be one to two months before I would get in to see him, depending on the urgency of need. A consultation for a possible surgery could be two months, but a follow-up visit after a recent surgery takes less than a month. So here again, there is not too much difference between the systems.

My primary care physician is much better, in that I can get an appointment with him, again depending on need, on that same day. However, this only happens during certain hours and if he has any openings. I am not sure how the public system works, whether it is just walk in and wait your turn or call for an appointment and hope for the best. But what all of my friends in both countries said was that the health care, when you do get it, is good.

In my research of this issue, talking and listening to other people speaking about its pros or cons, my overall view of the differences between the two types of systems comes down to how it is paid for by the citizens of the countries. Here in the United States, we have numerous health care insurance companies nationwide, and you look for the best (if you pay for your own), or you pay in your portion for the company your employer has contracted for to supply the health care insurance. In Canada and Great Britain, or any other countries with socialized health care, you pay taxes to the country that are out the door compared to our country's percentage. What may be our top income tax percentage for the richest of Americans might be the lowest percentage for the lowest income level in those countries. The flip side is we pay taxes to the government and pay at least a portion of our medical insurance too. They do not pay for medical insurance! We have to pay for any portion the insurance company does not cover on the medical bill. They don't!

I must admit that without sitting down and literally doing a side-by-side comparison of higher income taxes versus lower-income taxes and payments into a insurance plan (including paying that portion the insurance company does not cover), I cannot say which one of the systems is better or worse. In the use of common sense, we should do just that kind of side-by-side comparison. See how much Canadians pay in income taxes, taking an average low, medium, and high income; then compare that to the United States and the tax percentage for our low, medium, and high income earners and add in the national average of medical insurance payments between the employee and employer.

To get this answer, we would probably have to use advanced calculus. Once we did find someone who could handle this mathematical equation, then we would have to sit down and review that area I discussed earlier in this book about a flat (or referred to as a fair) tax or a NST. Then when all of the figures are in place, and we have recovered from the number crunching, a decision can be made on which system is the better for the family's financial bottom line. Remember, as far as the actual medical care, they are about the same.

Going back to my discussion on paying taxes in our country, I think I would rather pay a flat tax, or NST of 35 percent to the government and no health insurance payments. I currently pay over five thousand dollars a year for just my portion of my health insurance (which includes dental care). Add this to my income tax due as a family and it is very close, under the current income tax laws with all of the deductions, to what the Canadians or British are paying in taxes alone. Again, without the actual numbers to help me in this opinion, it looks to me that going with a flat tax, or NST, of 25 to 35 percent will result in a bigger take home for the family than today. By the way, that tax percentage I am talking about is both federal and state taxes combined, not just federal alone.

Using common sense here, why not look into a way to improve the average American's take-home pay? Let's adopt a 35 percent NST, which is my personal favored idea, and look at the fact that for every one million dollars spent in the United States, the federal and state governments would get three hundred fifty thousand dollars between them. Remember all of the overhead savings I detailed in the earlier chapter? Well, add no more health insurance payouts by the American family and we are even further ahead of where we were then. I am not endorsing socialism in any way, but when this kind of system can work in Canada and Great Britain (which are democracies too), maybe we should give this idea a fair and honest look. Here is another savings we would realize by going to a national health care system: no more Medicare provisions would have to be paid for by the federal government or Medicaid by the states. There is a few billion we could put into our coffers for other things.

Chapter 8

Short and Simple

Earlier, I mentioned the best way to write the legislation before our Congress would be to use the KISS method. But that should not be just on those issues before our government officials. In the last few decades, it seems that all of the legal documents have more legal lingo in them, and 90 percent of it cannot be understood without a law degree. I recently looked at a prospective contract, and it took over eleven pages to just say what I could have said in three pages. Because of today's world, judgments by juries, etc., you not only have to make sure you dot your I's and cross your T's, but you have to describe that you did in writing as well.

It is amazing how little lawyers can say, yet it takes two thousand five hundred–page bills like the recently passed health care legislation to say it. Completely different than this is our nation's Constitution and all of its amendments. If you contact your local Congressional representative's office, you can get a copy of the document in a little booklet that can be placed in your pocket or purse. How can our entire country operate on such a short document, which is the basis of all our laws and directs how our government works? It does not take a college education to figure this out; our Founding Fathers used the KISS method.

We declared our independence from England and fought two wars over a single-page document called the Declaration of Independence. Almost all of the amendments to the Constitution are less than a paragraph in length, yet they freed the slaves in the 1860's, outlawed and then reversed the ban on the production of alcoholic beverages, and in the case of the first ten, established our freedoms and rights as citizens of the United States. In the case of the Declaration of Independence and our Constitution and amendments, we as a country just simply stated the issue and kept the legal lingo out of them.

In the DOD, we have what we call a military specifications document, called a MILSPEC. This document provides the specifications for the different types of equipment. But the one that kills me was when one of my coworkers told me that he actually saw a MILSPEC for a toilet seat on a navy carrier that was over one hundred pages. Maybe that is why the darn things cost a king's ransom. I can only imagine how many pages the MILSPEC is for the whole carrier.

Now if we apply common sense to this chapter's issue, we can see the advantages to reforming our taxes in our country. Go with the flat tax, or the NST, and you eliminate all of those confusing tax forms, booklets, instructions, and problems with filing each year. What is so wrong with just simply stating the facts today?

When I listen to interviewers asking Congressional leaders questions, I get amused and then irritated with them. I do not believe a single person in our Congress, executive branch, or even some judicial members know how to simply answer a question. Instead, they go off on a tangent, start talking like a blubbering idiot, or all of a sudden get a memory lapse on the issue. I do not know who they are trying to impress, but it isn't me!

I remember the old television show *Dragnet*, and Sergeant Joe Friday's famous saying, "Give us the facts, just the facts." Even in law enforcement today, you have to read people their Miranda rights before you can ask them a simple question, or so it seems sometimes. Why don't we as a country just start telling like it is, stay with the facts, and tell the truth? It will be better for all of us. I do not want to be labeled with these idiots, so with this I end this chapter. See, short and simple!

Chapter 9

The Media Nonsense

In the late 1960's, the movie called *The Green Berets* that starred John Wayne included a newspaper reporter who was sent to Vietnam to bring back news that would reinforce the nation's feelings against the war. This was not just Hollywood creating a part in a movie. It happened to be a fact across the print and broadcast media during that time. The war was not popular (what war is?), and instead of the media putting on the best for our soldiers who were trying to prevent the expansion of communism into South Vietnam, they pounced, literally, on the antiwar sentiments in the United States.

The historical newsreels, the "MovieTone" news clips seen in movie theaters across the nation during World War II and the Korean War, and the fair coverage of these wars changed dramatically in the Vietnam War coverage and ever since. All of a sudden, the soldiers were the bad guys. They were doing terrible things to people, and the news organizations were following people like Jane Fonda who traveled to North Vietnam in their protests against the war. When the Vietnam War was over, our soldiers got a reception of ridiculing words, got spit upon, and were treated like dirt.

I grew up during the Vietnam War and missed being drafted by only one year. However, I have several friends who did serve in that war, and the Vietnam Veteran's Memorial Wall in Washington DC has the names of 58,267 (as of the addition of six names in 2010) of the soldiers and sailors who served in that war and gave their lives in the service of our country. If you have never seen the wall, you need to go there! On the three or four occasions I was there, I never left without crying, nor have many others. I do not know if it still is, since the opening of the World War II Memorial, but at one time the wall was the most-visited place in Washington DC. During the 2010 Rolling Thunder motorcycle ride by Vietnam vets in Washington, two men who attend my church were riding by and saw a currently serving Marine standing at one of the street corners saluting all of them. Where was the media covering this event?

Well, today's media does not look for these kind of things, because they are too busy looking for some kind of dirty laundry on a Congressional member, the president, or some other famous person or organization. They cannot show a Marine crying, expressing his pride in those who went before him, but they will show protestors in San Francisco raising all kinds of dust because men cannot marry other men and women cannot marry other women. Talk about your messed-up values. The media needs a good house cleaning of itself.

Maybe I was born on the wrong side of the tracks, but why would you not want to find and tell about those things and events that build up our country? Despite all of the adverse things in our country, that Marine had his values in order, and I am very proud of his service to the United States. However, the media cannot spell, nor can it seem to use, common sense either. We have enough people in this country who want to take down that which our Founding Fathers created, so we do not need any help from the very organizations that were established to keep the citizens informed.

During the early years of our country, a person called a town crier would come out at certain times and read notices or news to the citizens of that town or village in an attempt to keep the people informed. Later, the print media started up and printed newspapers for distribution to the public for the same purpose. Except for a few dimwits, the media was a trusted source of information up to the time of the 1960's, and then things went downhill fast. Why? Someone decided that it was not news unless it defamed a person, told the bad side only, or did all it could to tear down our country's values.

The media was all over Madelyn Murray O'Hair (a well-known atheist activist and member of the American Communist party) when she brought her suit to the United States Supreme Court (Murray vs. Curlett) in 1963 to remove prayer and Bible reading from the schools. But did you ever hear anything about the people on the other side of that argument before that court? How about the court ruling on Roe vs. Wade (1973) that legalized abortion in the United States. So who was Wade? The point is that the media is only bringing out one side of an issue, and that is the one they usually want to see succeed.

How could anyone forget the obvious bias on the part of several major news organizations, both print and broadcast, and that of certain television personalities supporting the presidential candidacy of now President Barack Obama? Some were just about tripping over themselves trying to see who could make him, then-candidate Obama, look like the only choice. Then there was the overly biased support, mainly based on the fact that he was African American. Again, the point here was that media sources were doing whatever it took to sway the voters on who they said needed to be the next president.

Let me insert a plain statement at this point. I do not care if my president is Caucasian, African American, Latin American, or Native American; I just want him or her to be a fair and just person, with high integrity. Anymore I feel that whoever the media wants in office is just the person we should vote against. No matter what they claim, the media wants them in office, because they have an alternative motive other than the country's best interest in mind.

Another notable swaying by the media concerns things having to do with Christianity in our country. They were all over the ACLU's drive to prevent retailers from saying, "Merry Christmas" and their threats to sue any retailer who allowed their employees to do so. But except for Mr. Bill O'Reilly from FoxNews, none of them exposed this action for what it really was, an attempt to remove Christ from the holiday season. However, my man Bill suggested a boycott of any retailers who did not allow their employees to say "Merry Christmas," and as I stated earlier in this book, the boycott got the retailers right where it hurt most, in their bottom line.

Here is what needs to be required of the media, and that is the plain facts of the given issue. The coverage should provide both sides of the issue, giving equal time to opinions, fair hearing of the comments, a detailed review of the background on an issue, and any additional information. One of the things I like about FoxNews is that they put out the facts, and then they tell us, the viewers, to decide for ourselves. Sure, let the imams from Islam have their say, but give equal time to people like Franklin Graham, Dr. Charles Stanley, and others. Then let the people decide whether a nativity scene will remain on public display or not, not the media.

Finally, it is time for us as citizens of this country to demand fair media coverage of events. The media should be the first to use their influence to maintain our civil rights as set forth in the Constitution and the Bill of Rights. When attempts are being made to deny a person the right to say "Merry Christmas," the media should be all over this attempt to deny a person his or her freedom of speech as provided in the First Amendment to the Constitution. They seem to be favoring this socialist agenda of President Obama, but if socialism really gets a hold on in this country, they will not be able to print or broadcast anything without previous permission, like it was in the Soviet Union of years past. Wake up, media, common sense should tell you to give us the facts and only the facts.

Chapter 10

If You Don't Vote, Don't Complain

When the Constitution of the United States was written, it was not perfect. After all, a human being wrote it, so in no way would it be perfect. That is why, since it was approved, it has been amended twenty-seven times, as of this writing. The fifteenth amendment gave the right to vote to all men of color in 1870, and the nineteenth amendment gave the right to vote to women in 1920.

Whether it has been from the beginning of our country, when only the white men could vote, or since the right to vote was granted to all citizens, no matter their gender or color, the greatest civic duty and right of all Americans has been our vote. Each person gets one vote for each office, proposed legislation, or proposition on the ballot. The majority of the votes cast determine the outcome of that election for office or proposed action by the governing body.

I have already addressed the issue of judges overruling the voters earlier in this book, so I will let that stand for itself. However, in this chapter I want to deal with those of you who have this idea that your vote will not count, so why bother. To my knowledge, there is only one place in our country where all members must vote unanimously, and that is on a jury. Otherwise, majority rules the day.

In 1972, the Congress and then-President Richard Nixon established the minimum voting age as eighteen years old, and it just so happened that was the year I turned eighteen, so I got to vote in that year's presidential election. Maybe it was just because it was my first time, but I felt a great deal of pride to be able to express my desire for our country's future when I entered that voting booth. I pushed down my selections, pulled back the machine arm, and knew that I had at least input my votes.

I do not care that over one hundred million votes can be involved in a national election; I believe that my one vote is a personal statement. I might be part of the minority that lost, but my vote was in there. Those of you who do not vote because you are convinced that your one vote makes no difference are just denying yourselves the most powerful right you have as a citizen. Why would you want to do that, and not make a statement of your own?

I believe the most *Critical Condition* in this country is complacency on the part of voters on Election Day. Do you remember the 2004 presidential election results? The SP folks, far lefters, and ultra liberals were incensed about the fact that the conservative Christians came out in such a large way and helped to re-elect George W. Bush to a second term as president. However, just the opposite happened in 2008. The conservative folks stayed home (for reasons I cannot understand), and we ended up with a far left liberal president. I can hear it now, but he won by several million votes. Yep, but if you several million who stayed home had voted, he would still be a senator, and Senator John McCain would be our president, and then-Governor Sarah Palin would be our vice president. Don't say maybe, that is a fact! Remember, majority rules the day when we vote. Also, do not concern yourselves if someone else did not vote; just make sure you do and make your vote count.

Recently, the lack of conservative/right-wing voters cost the students of the Dover, Pennsylvania, school district the right to have Intelligent Design (Creation) taught in their schools. The voters could choose between potential board members who favored the inclusion of

Intelligent Design and those who intended to prevent it being taught in the schools at all. The candidates who wanted to prevent it from the school curriculum won the day, but many of those who were upset about the outcome had only themselves to blame for not getting out there and voting.

I am getting tired of hearing, "I have only one vote." Well, so does everybody else! I feel it is my civic duty to get out and vote, and I want people to see that I did. For fame? No, for the reason that I am and will continue to exercise my right as a citizen to do so. Okay, I will be fair and admit that your vote may be one in several million, but that is on a national or on a state level. How about those local school board elections, city or town council, or county commissioner decisions? Your one vote counts, no matter what it is cast for or for whom. I make it well known that I did not vote for President Barack Obama, so no one can look at me and ask where my vote was on that Election Day. Make it a point the next time get out and vote. Exercise this right, and thank the Lord above you have this right. There are many countries in this world where voting is either nonexistent or can be deadly if you try.

Chapter 11

A Mosque near "Ground Zero"

FACT: Everybody and every organization has the right, under the Constitution, to worship and establish a place of worship where they wish as long as the location is in accordance with the laws and ordinances of that town, city, county, or state.

The use of common sense will tell you if something is right or wrong, will benefit your fellow Americans, and most importantly will bring honor and glory to our creator. Some things can be overlooked, because they are not a big deal, are not worth the effort required to change them, or do not offend other people in any way. However, the proposed mosque and cultural center near "Ground Zero" in New York City (site of the September 11, 2001, attacks) does not fit into this description.

On that horrible day in history, Islamic extremists took two commercial aircraft, crashed them into two of the most important buildings in the financial world, and killed thousands of innocent people. I would guess that less than 1 percent of the people in the first building to be hit even saw what was coming or even know to this day what happened to them. But those in the second building, after already seeing what happened next to them, went through horror that is probably impossible to describe when they saw the second plane coming at them.

In addition to those who lost their lives in New York City (both the workers in the buildings and the rescue heroes), we cannot forget those of our military and civilians working at the Pentagon, and all of the people on the planes themselves, who perished on that horrible day. Todd Beamer and his fellow passengers on Flight 93 are national heroes in my opinion, because they prevented further damage and death in the Washington DC area, or so the experts feel was the target of that particular aircraft.

Since that fateful day, several attempts to inflict harm on this country by Al Qaeda and their related factions have been prevented, and I give God Almighty the whole credit for this fact. God either prevented the success of the terrorist actions or gave our intelligence community, and just plain folks on the planes and other locations, special wisdom and awareness to identify and stop the attacks. But the Islamic terrorists keep trying, and I am afraid they will again be successful.

Construction is currently underway to build a memorial to those who lost their lives at Ground Zero, and I feel this is a very justified action on the part of our country. In the early stages of planning for this memorial, or so I am told, someone suggested that two of the metal girders used in the construction of the towers be used to form a cross and make them a part of that memorial design. (Just after the attack of September 11, 2001, the rescue workers at Ground Zero made a cross out of some of the broken girders.) You can imagine what happened to that suggestion in short order, and that is a shame. That cross should have been approved and made the center point of the whole memorial. But no, we cannot do that because it might offend someone from the Muslim community. It is this kind of thinking that proves to be that being politically correct has gone too far in our country.

If a person wants to become and follow the Islamic religion, that is his or her choice, but why are we so afraid of offending people with a Christian symbol? The proposed mosque and cultural center near "Ground Zero" offends me, but will that prevent it from being built?

Well I certainly hope so but probably not. What I want to know is why? There is not even an ounce of common sense in allowing the building of the Muslim facility in that area. Nor are the city or mayor of New York City being fair or reasonable on this situation. On the day of that horrible attack, the nearby Greek Orthodox Church was destroyed, and New York City has yet to grant them a rebuilding permit, as of this writing. Why?

In New York City and in other parts of our country, several honor killings by Muslim parents on their daughters (just because they dated non-Muslim boys) have occurred. So why are we afraid of offending these people? I will tell you why; we are afraid of them attacking us again. The way our country is bending over backward to prevent racial profiling on the Arab-Americans is just plain silly and needs to be stopped. They are no more important than other Americans, and they need to stop these idiotic claims of this place or that place being holy as designated by the American Ayatollah, who is at this time hiding somewhere in Yemen. In the Islamic religion, a place that is designated as holy must have a mosque placed upon it. But Ground Zero is not holy in Muslim terms. It is more like the location where the greatest example of hatred was carried out, and to desecrate it with a Muslim facility is crossing the line.

There are already quite a few mosques in the greater New York City area, so there is no justified reason to build one at this location but to rub into the Americans' noses the fact that Islam struck us here. The decision to build this facility of hate on this site should be decided by the voters of New York City, and that vote would be final. A vote should also be held on whether a cross from the girders from the towers will be on the memorial site and not by those afraid of offending those who attacked us.

How about this idea? Until the state of New York, and specifically New York City, agrees to allow the voters to decide these issues, the rest of us Americans will boycott the city and stop bringing our tourist dollars to their theater district and anywhere else in and around that part of New York. Once the voters have made the decision, no court will overrule the decision just because someone did not get their way in the election. If this happens, then we as a nation should step in by requiring a national referendum that would be binding upon whether a mosque goes up or stays up, if it has been already built by that time.

Just think if nobody showed up for the Macy's Thanksgiving Day parade. Businesses would choose to move their offices out of New York, actors and actresses would refuse to perform in the city, and so on. Not to mention, this is a nation established on Judeo-Christian values. We cannot allow Islam to run our country anymore than we can allow our government officials to tell the religious community how and when we can worship and to whom we will bring our worship. You may not feel I am being fair on this issue at all, but where do we draw the line with the Muslim community? Do we also let them declare the attack on the Pentagon and the crash site of Flight 93 in Stonycreek Township, near Shanksville, Pennsylvania, as holy land so mosques can be built their too?

Chapter 12

The Immigration Issue

In New York City's harbor is Liberty Island, home to the Statue of Liberty. Nearby is Ellis Island, where several million of our citizens today had family members enter into the United States as immigrants from other countries. My dad tells a very old joke about the immigration process. A tall gentleman from Norway came up to the counter to be processed, and the immigration official asked him his name. "Jon Johnson" (pronounced Yon Yonson), he booms with a very strong Norwegian accent. The official finishes the processing, and the next person to walk up was a very short immigrant from the Orient. "What is your name?" the official asked. "Sim Ting," said the immigrant. So the official processes him in as Jon Johnson. Okay, not so funny, but I guess you would have had to be there.

In many countries, including the United States, there is a defined process for immigrating into the country. However, today we are dealing with those who are entering illegally and in doing so are bringing across illegal drugs, committing crimes, and taking jobs away from those who live here in accordance with the rules of the land. In my earlier chapter on using our military for our defense, I addressed this issue, but I feel we need to expand it a little. Between our borders with Canada and Mexico, we have the longest common borders between countries in the world. The border between the

United States and Mexico is over two thousand miles long, and between the United States and Canada it is in excess of four thousand miles, including the border between Canada and the state of Alaska. They are also the longest peaceful borders in the world.

Lately, people from many different countries, not just Mexico and Canada, have been using these borders to illegally enter our country. Believe it or not, and I hope Mr. Ripley will excuse me using that statement, there are places on both borders where you cannot tell if you are in the United States or the other country. Several crossings are just small, two-lane roads, and the majority of the borders are just flat land. The responsibility of guarding our borders and shorelines belongs to the DHS. Those entities charged with performing this function are the US Coast Guard (USCG) and the Border Patrol. Also involved, in a smaller way, are the Immigration Customs Enforcement (ICE), the Drug Enforcement Agency (DEA), and the local law enforcement agencies.

The problem is that all of these entities combined cannot guard every inch of our borders and shorelines with the current manpower they have today. As I stated before, the Border Patrol has about one person for every ten miles of border with Mexico. Even with the modern technology of the unmanned drone, some movement sensors, and the few miles where a fence does exist, the officials are simply undermanned and underfunded.

I recently heard that we are fast approaching the one trillion-dollar mark in funding our military's involvements in Iraq and Afghanistan. If we spent just one fourth of that on funding and manning our borders, we would not be having the immigration problems of today. However, our naive president believes that our borders are more secure than they have ever been, with the personnel we have out there at this time. Boy is his head in the sand on this one! The DHS secretary, Janet Napolitano, is mainly responsible for this statement, because she would not recognize a problem if it walked past her. Also, she was one of the first in President Obama's administration to criticize the new Arizona immigration law.

The real problem the Obama administration has with the Arizona law is that it trumped them before they acted on this issue. It is not a new police action to ask a person for his or her identification papers when being stopped for a violation. Here in Pennsylvania, you must provide the officer your driver's license, car registration, and verification of insurance. Failure to do so will result in a fine on top of that for which you were stopped. This racial profiling claim is just another way for people to get out of being charged for criminal activity, similar to that when they claim their Miranda rights were not provided to them in time. This is idiotic, and the police are being limited even more by these lame-brained accusations. Law enforcement officers today are having to be lawyers, as well as performing their charged duties, just to prevent someone from getting the charges dismissed on some puny detail.

Yes, a person is innocent until proven guilty, but that does not mean a person does not have to have some kind of identification on him or her. I carry an identification that has both my picture and that of my guide dog on it, to prove that Jodi is a guide dog and is permitted into places like restaurants, etc. Without it, I could claim this fact all day, but without the proof, I am just wasting my breath. The same goes for a person claiming his or her place of residency (i.e., state, city, address of residency, and other information). The only difference the Arizona law has with this is that it requires the law enforcement community to perform this function. If the truth be known, they probably have been doing it all along. It was just put onto paper, and now people are raising all kinds of stupid complaints about the law.

Again, our current government officials are not using common sense here. When a police officer, whether he or she be local, state, or federal in level of enforcement, needs to know who he or she is talking to, if the vehicle a person is operating belongs to him or her, and any other information that would help in the performance of his or her civil duties, then requesting a person's identification should be considered as acceptable. When police officers are being denied this ability, we are asking to bury quite a few more of them in the future. The correct thing to do, and the most sensible too, is to allow the law enforcement department to do just that, enforce the law, and whatever comes out of that action is just the way it goes. Get caught committing a crime, do the time. Instead, we are encouraging these lowlifes to shout out racial profiling, and the nutcases who are running our country today are buying it in the courts.

Chapter 13

Wake Up, People of the World

I have referred to the United States all through this book, but I want all of the readers to know that common sense does not belong to us Americans only. The use of common sense is, and should be, international. No matter where you are in the world, there must come a time when you just sit down with your coworkers, partners in business, family, and/or friends and just brainstorm out the issues and problems facing your company, personal life, or country. No one person has all of the answers, nor should we as citizens of the world follow such a person, because he or she will lead us down the wrong path eventually.

Also, we have addressed several issues, looked at alternatives, and given both sides as fair a hearing as we can, and now we need to bring all of this to a close. However, before we do this, we need to look at some of the issues again, in a brief way, and some other issues not addressed up to this point. In every case, we need to start using and demanding our leaders also use simple common sense in the matters of our country and interests.

I feel the main reason common sense is not used today is because it prevents some from their liberal agendas. They are looking to obtain fame and power and influence people in ways that make them look good, increase their status in the public eye, and cause the world to spin in accordance with their idea of how things should be in our lives and country. Instead, common sense undermines this type of thinking, and that is why it is so lacking in our world today.

Except for some smaller issues, occasions, and events, this world has not stopped and said that this or that situation is just not acceptable. In World War II, the three persons who caused this world to regress into that very costly war, Hitler, Mussolini, and Hirohito, were those kind of people who were thought to have all of the answers, and the result was a totally destroyed Europe, two atom bombs on Japan, and over 20 million dead worldwide. As we bring this to a close, let's decide here and now that before we simply follow someone and jump off the cliff too, we will sit down, talk, and discuss the issue and any options and definitely apply common sense to the final decision. Until we do, we will continue to have the many wars, terrorist actions, and just plain stupidity in this world we have today.

A Simplified Tax

When was the last time you gave the 1040 tax form, also referred to as the long form, a good look and review? There are lines on that form for types of income, types of tax deferred income, and deductions that I have never heard of and probably never will understand. In addition, there are IRS publications for just about every one of the lines too. Add to this the Schedules A, B, C, D, and on it goes for specialized incomes or deductions.

Our Congress debates and lobbyists do all they can to influence what the tax laws will be for the next tax year. All kinds of legal lingo goes flying through the halls of Congress, and once the final product is agreed upon, our government printing offices go into high gear pumping out the forms and publications for us taxpayers to fill in and return.

Well this is just plain nuts and shows a lack of wanting to help the public on the part of our Congress. Why they do not see the benefits of a simplified tax law and subsequent forms is beyond my understanding. I think it must be part of parliamentary rules to not do things sensibly. The cost savings to our government for not having to reprint all those tax forms each year, because of the many or few changes enacted by Congress, would be in the millions of dollars. Not to mention all of the trees we would be saving in the forests (that is for my environmental friends and readers). But on top of that, filing would be so simple that probably 75 percent, at least, of the IRS employees would not be needed, and the buildings they work in and that are maintained nationwide could be closed.

Furthermore, in this day and age of home computers, people would be able to file their income taxes much easier and quicker. If all you have to show is the gross income you received for the past year, enter the income taxes withheld that year, and list the income tax burden based on the established percentage, it would take just a few minutes to do the annual requirement of each and every citizen. At the bottom of the form, you would list the refund or tax due, and if the total is less than a dollar, the payment or refund would be waived. This would apply to those states who have an income tax as well and to the local taxing agencies too. We really need to apply the KISS method to our tax laws. If we don't, the confusion, tax loopholes, and numerous people who do not have to pay any taxes will just continue. But then there is my NST idea.

I am more convinced now than I was when writing about this issue earlier that an NST instead of an income tax would be better for us as a country and the citizens. The most important thing would be that everybody pays. No more giving a large amount to charity to avoid paying any taxes, no more tax evasion, and everyone would pay the same. In addition, I know that everybody will bring home more money to spend, and this will help increase our economy, create new jobs, and bring down the deficit.

Health Care

I have almost pounded this issue to death, but I want to say a little bit more on this matter. We are spending billions each year for our health care, be it our payments from each check and our employer's payment, the part the insurance companies do not cover, or the Medicare and Medicaid payments from the government. Something has just got to give on this issue, and the new health care legislation passed in May of 2010 is not the answer.

Without knowing the details, all of the underlying issues, and most importantly how it would affect each family, I must again state that I would like to see us at least give a fair and accurate look at a national health system. We would have to be allowed to select our own doctors, family physicians, surgeons, and other types of medical, dental, and eye specialists; and the benefits of going this way would mean health care for all. We might be able to eliminate Medicare and Medicaid too.

How would we pay for this? Simple, use the KISS method again. The government would establish an NST, say thirty-five cents for every dollar spent, and this money would cover the federal, state, and local funding for all departments and services. However, the medical world would have to buy into this proposal too. Doctors, hospitals, and other areas of this field would not just be able to bill at the rate they feel the service requires. Instead, a set fee would be established for a visit to the physician, dentist, or eye professional. The same would be applied to surgery charges, hospital room care, and on it goes. Folks, this is doable, but we as a nation must be willing to accept change. In addition to these kinds of changes, review boards would be responsible for keeping check on doctors and weeding out the quacks, and the malpractice suits would be history.

Maybe I am way off base on this one, but don't throw out an idea until it has been given a fair testing, review, and most of all, approval by the voters of the United States. Just because a method of health care is referred to as a social system does not make it a bad one. Remember, we call our retirement system Social Security. The point is, and I do not have all of the answers either, that we as a country are going to have to deal with our fourteen trillion dollar and growing deficit soon, or we are going to go bankrupt as a nation. God help us when our foreign creditors come looking for their money invested in our country. Have you practiced your Chinese lately?

Also, why not ask the Canadians to give us the methods they undertook on establishing their system, and try them out here? Who said we have all of the answers as a nation either? If a system works, let's look into it, research its ups and downs and positives and negatives, and then put all of the evidence before the people for their decision. Prior to bringing the proposal to change to a vote, let's have many many town halls for the citizens to ask questions, bring up options, brainstorm the issue, and develop the system and its cost. If you involve the rank and file of the citizens, you will see a much better way of bringing about change, and they will be much better informed on the details so as to make their decision in the voting booth.

No More Earmarks

In listening to the news, I heard the celebrities on a news show talking about and listing some of the most ridiculous payments made out from our government. However, the one that just about put me away was an urgent payment requirement by a university researcher for $180,000 to study the effects of freezing rat sperm. *What?* The worst part of this is that the payment was made by our government out of the almost eight hundred billion-dollar stimulus bill.

In the past, I have heard of funded studies on the environmental effects of cow belching, threats on the kelp forests in the ocean, and many other totally useless expenditures by our Congress on their special budgetary requests or amendments to bills, earmarks. This is going to have to stop. If we are going to reel in our economy and spending by our governmental leaders, this will be the first place to start. Funding road repairs, replacing a bridge in dire need of repair or replacement, new and improved traffic lights, and any other beneficial projects to the public are one thing, but studying the effects on freezing rat sperm is another. Who cares? These boondoggles cost us as taxpayers billions each year, and the benefits are nothing. I could be selfish and demand a public transit system be established where I live so I can get to work each day without depending on a carpool, but that won't fly. Why? It makes too much sense, and we cannot do that in our government.

Ever wonder if your Congressional representative or senator submitted one of these stupid and idiotic funding requests? Well, just ask for a copy of his or her Congressional record. It is public information, and you can bet if they know the people are going to start checking up on them, this crap is going to stop. The alternative, of course, will be that their tenure in Congress will be shortened at the next election.

Then there are the people who are submitting these totally ridiculous requests. They may think they are important, but you are going to have to come up with some kind of presentation to justify funding research on freezing rat sperm to me. Where are the scientists on researching safe and efficient ways of dealing with spent nuclear rods from our country's nuclear reactors? What about developing the hydrogen-fueled car for mass production by the car makers? Why aren't we fielding more and more wind turbines to power our cities and towns? These would be good funding projects for Congress to approve, because they would benefit all of us in many ways, improve the environment, and help us to be more energy independent of foreign countries.

Maybe we need our medical researchers to find out what the disease is that prevents some people from even spelling common sense, not to mention using it. Many of the ideas, suggestions, and theories I have put forth in this book have come from my simple mind. Others came from experience and knowledge of the issue, knowing that the benefits would be great and the savings even greater. People, you need to get rid of the cobwebs in your head and start using the gray matter God gave us to benefit the country.

Put Prayer and Bible Reading Back into the Schools

In 1963, we had one great occurrence in that my wife Lori was born in December of that year. However, we had two very bad occurrences during that same year. In November, we lost President John F. Kennedy to an assassin's bullet. But earlier that year, the moral standards of our country started downward with the Supreme Court ruling that banned prayer and Bible reading from the schools. I remember very well hearing the Scripture reading of the day and the prayer being spoken over the loudspeaker system while at Wilson Elementary School in San Antonio, Texas. Then later that year, all we heard was the announcements and nothing else. Before when the Bible was being read and the prayers spoken, many of the kids in my class did or did not pay attention, depending on their personal convictions. Then after they stopped, nothing changed in the classroom. The same kids would listen or ignore the announcements in the same way they listened or ignored the Bible reading and prayers. Up to that time, if the kids wanted to listen they did, and if they did not, they just ignored them.

So why did we have to have the Supreme Court rule that prayer and Bible reading must be removed from the schools? Well, some lady from Austin, Texas, sued to have it removed, and our nation's highest court bowed to one person's complaint about this morning activity and ruled it was unconstitutional. Cowards! Just because one person does not like something does not mean it should affect the whole nation, especially when most either listened or could not have cared less.

The appropriate thing that the Supreme Court should have done was order the voters on a national level to decide if prayer and Bible reading will be allowed in the schools. Because they did not let the voters decide it then, I call upon Congress to allow the citizens of the United States to decide if prayer, Bible reading and clubs, and any religious activity may be held in our schools. Once the vote is taken, it is final.

"Merry Christmas," Not Winter Holiday

Every year during the Christmas season, my carpool driver and I always look forward to hearing the comedic rendition of the "Twelve Pains of Christmas." We laugh our guts out at that song, even though we have heard it hundreds of times. There are so many songs and jingles written for that particular time of year, and most of them refer to the Christ child in some way or another. Songs like "O Little Town of Bethlehem," "Away in a Manger," "What Child Is This," and many more are all heard at that time and usually by several different performers.

Enter the idiots from the ACLU. They are so dedicated to removing Christ, or any references to God, Jesus, and any other types of items or words that point to their existence that they threaten to sue people or retailers for saying, "Merry Christmas." These far left-leaning folks probably spell common with a K. So what, we now have to call it the twelve pains of the winter holiday?

I have heard that efforts to enforce this demand may go as far as charging a person who says the "Merry Christmas" greeting with having committed a crime punishable by jail time. Now how nutty can they get? Obviously, they can get quite nutty! That will be the day that I go to jail for exercising my freedom of speech by saying, "Merry Christmas." I will shout so loud in the Supreme Court building that the roof will be launched into orbit with the International Space Station (ISS).

Come on, people of the United States, and the world, for that matter; letting these idiots tell you what you can and cannot say, and when you can say it, needs to be dealt with once and for all. Start raising your own fuss. Protest the denial of a school play that refers to God, any attempts to stop the placing of a nativity in a public place, stopping people from singing Christmas carols in public, demanding that Christmas be changed to winter holiday on the calendars, or any other actions to remove God and Jesus Christ from our country. They do not own the holiday, we do, so say, "Merry Christmas" as often as you can and to as many people as you can.

Display Your American Flag Proudly

I don't know how many of you have ever had the opportunity to come to Washington DC for a visit, but a couple of days at the Smithsonian are a must, whether it is the very famous display of the Hope Diamond and the other precious gems in the Natural History Museum or the Air and Space Museum (which is the most visited of all the Smithsonian buildings). But the one I want to address in this section is the American History Museum. When you first enter this museum, you are immediately captured by the huge pendulum swinging in the center of the building. But even more important is what is kept behind the wall beyond the pendulum.

During the War of 1812, while off shore on a British warship as a prisoner, a gentleman by the name of Francis Scott Key was observing the battle at Fort McHenry near Baltimore, Maryland. Bombs were blowing up all over the place, smoke was everywhere, and the sounds of the battle were all around him. Then just for a moment, he was able to get a glimpse of the Fort, and through all of the smoke and fire, he saw the flag of the United States still flying over the Fort. His first reaction was to take out a piece of paper, and he began to write a poem. Today we know it as our national anthem, called the "Star-Spangled Banner." At scheduled times in the American History Museum, the wall behind that pendulum will open to reveal a very large and beaten up flag. But not just any flag; it is the Star-Spangled Banner, the very flag that Francis Scott Key saw from that British warship. The presentation takes the observer through the many versions of the anthem up to how it is performed today.

I do not know how you feel about it, but that song always sends a chill up my back with pride in what we have as a nation. It, along with songs like the "Stars and Stripes Forever," "America the Beautiful," "The Battle Hymn of the Republic," and "God Bless America," makes this guy very grateful for the freedoms we have but so fearful that so many in our nation are trying to degrade them or even remove them completely. Our Judeo-Christian standards are under so much attack today that anything that refers to God,

Jesus Christ, the cross, or anything Christian is in danger of being removed from us as (believe it or not) unconstitutional.

We have already had an attempt made to remove, "One nation, under God…" from our Pledge of Allegiance, the SP folks want "In God We Trust" removed from our money, and all over the country the folks from the AUSCS are threatening to sue if public displays of the Ten Commandments are not removed. So what is next, deleting the fourth verse of the "Star-Spangled Banner"? That fourth verse ends with these words: "In God is our trust."

By removing God from our country, you undermine the very foundation our Founding Fathers set forth for us as a nation. Why would someone want to degrade the very freedoms that allow them to protest? Without them, we would be like the oppressed peoples of China, North Korea, Cuba, and other totalitarian ruled countries. Sometimes those people cannot sneeze without permission from their respective governments.

I fly my American flag in front of my home quite often, and mainly to show my pride in my country. It is my way of telling others that I am a loyal American, and to those who would degrade our nation, that they better not mess with the people who live at this place. I defend my country and our belief in God; however, I am irritated at those Christians who feel they should not express loyalty to the United States. Fly the flag, and honor our country!

Meet with Your Congressional Representatives and/or Senators

Have you ever said that you do not like that our country is doing this or that and wondered what you could do about it? I know the answer. Make contact with the people who are elected to represent you in Washington, your state capital, or your local governing bodies. They are there because you, the voters, put them there, and you can take them out of there too. On many occasions, these officials will hold town hall meetings. These meetings are held to bring you up to date on the latest legislation before their respective legislative bodies, proposals in committee, and to get and listen to concerns from you, the citizens they represent. If one is coming up soon, be there; if not, ask for one to be held.

Previously, I stated that the past Congress, and some current Congressional members, do not seem to care what we the voters think about and like or do not like. They just seem to go off on tangents until they get their way. The problem is that it is not supposed to be their way; it is supposed to be our way. So why do we as voters just keep re-electing these dimwits? When I hear a nut case like Representative Barney Frank (D-Massachusetts) stating that we should legalize marijuana in the same way tobacco is legal, my blood begins to boil. This kind of donut-hole thinking has no place in our country. Then there was her majesty Representative Nancy Pelosi (D-California), who lost her position as speaker of the House of Representatives as a result of the 2010 elections. She on several occasions made it clear that the nation will change to her way of thinking, and too bad if the people do not like it. What? Who represents who here?

So what do you do if your representative does not respond to the wishes of the people? Go to the voting booth and boot his or her butt out of there. If no one will run against him or her, do it yourself. And this does not just apply to our Congress folks in Washington; this can be done on the state and local levels too. If the county commissioners are taxing you to death, run against them and change the way things are going at that level of government. The point I am making here is simple: they either represent us or they can join those members of Congress who were removed as a result of the 2010 midterm elections.

One more thing: in today's world, most, if not all, of our representatives have their own websites where you can send them a message, comment, and show your displeasures about how things and issues are being handled. Utilize that site for current information, to find out the status of some kind of legislation, or to communicate your feelings on a certain subject. Bottom line, let these folks know what you want them to do for you, or kick them out of office!

No Is No, So What Part of No Do You Not Understand?

I will speak for myself, but I am fed up with judges in this country overruling the law of this land from the bench. In addition, who do they think they are overruling the voters? I had a T-shirt at one time that said, "What Part of NO Did You Not Understand, Was it the N or the O?" Every time I hear of a judge, or a group of judges, making these rulings that overrule the majority, I just lose it. We live in a democracy where the majority rules the day. If voters in a state say no to giving insurance benefits to same-sex partners, then that should be it, but no. In today's world, if you don't get your way from the voters, you just sue, claiming the law violates your civil rights, and the judges throw out the law as unconstitutional or discriminatory. Let me be short and direct to the point on this issue. If we the voters say no, it is *"no!"*

Now it is time we settle this thing about who is in charge in this country and who answers to whom. I have hammered away on the use of common sense all through this book, and it is, and always will be, a fact that using common sense does not change over time. What was sensible in 1776 is still that way today.

Chapter 14

It Is Spelled with a C

I think we have just about beaten this issue on the lack of common sense in America to death. For sure, our leaders need to get on the stick and get back to doing what they were sent to our seats of government to do, and that is representing the interests and desires of the voters. But how many times do we have to tell them that is why they are in these positions? So many books have come out recently from former Governors Sarah Palin and Mike Huckabee, Karl Rove, Bill O'Reilly, and Dick Morris; and in every case, they have exposed our recently past Congress, some in our current Congress, and others for pursuing their own agendas and not that of the voters.

Some things are just plain wrong, and you do not need a four-year college degree to know that it is wrong. The problem is, sadly, that many of the SP folks, ACLU, AUUSCS, and other organizations with a far left liberal tilt simply want it their way. The majority may not like it, the laws of our land say it is illegal, or just basic thinking would tell you it is wrong. However, they cannot allow their agendas to be stopped by something like common sense.

So what do we do when they do not listen? Several ideas come to mind. We are a Judeo-Christian founded nation, so let's get on our knees and pray for our country, its leaders, and each and every one of us. We need to stop these outright attempts and intentional actions to remove anything about God, Jesus Christ, and anything else Christian from the very fabric of our nation. Our Congress needs to start listening to the people and not just the few idiots who throw around lobbyist money like it is snowing dollar bills. Finally, it is not their agenda, it is supposed to be the people's agenda that they are to be working on and pursuing in the halls of government.

On top of all of these far left agendas, we need to rein in the rulings and decisions that are permitting the downhill slide of our morals in this country. Our schools today are campuses of disrespect for the teachers, and the kids come out just as ignorant as they were when they went in, unable to read a lick, and are dumber than some dogs I know in the area. The administrators are so afraid of being sued by one of the far left gangs that even wearing a cross as a necklace cannot be allowed, but the girls can wear skirts up to their butts and show ten miles of cleavage. You don't even have to go to porn websites for naked women anymore; just turn on the television and cruise through the cable channels. There is even a game show where topless women can be seen without any warning to the viewers.

In our everyday life, things are just simply screwed up. If the ACLU gets its way, eventually you will be put in jail for saying, "Merry Christmas," but someone can use profane language in public and that is perfectly acceptable. Even in places where you would think people should give consideration to their words you will hear the F- words fly, girls will sit down at restaurant tables and spread their legs to reveal themselves, and guys will just plain violate women in the mall without any fear of reprisals. I pity some of the girls who do want to be proper because they are usually the ones who get their breasts grabbed or their skirts lifted by other boys and girls alike. What is wrong with this world? The answer here is just as simple: God is not at the center of our family lives, work places, interrelationships in public places, and the very fabric of everything we say and do.

This nation has a disease of moral degradation, lowering of moral standards, and most of all taking actions to remove God from everything in our lives ever since that stupid ruling in 1963. People, we need to straighten up. If we are going to change our country back to the moral and upright nation our Founding Fathers envisioned as, it will have to start with each and every one of us. We need to get ourselves into a good, Bible-teaching church every Sunday. We need to start acting like a people of high moral standards, and treat each other with respect and honor each other's wishes for space and/or the ability to do our everyday duties without having to look over our shoulders for fear of being attacked or robbed. So how do we start? Think about your question. What would common sense tell you to do first? I will give you a hint: look in a mirror. It starts with you and me and goes from there. If you want to make a change in this world, be the place where it started. Then do all you can to make it spread like the flu virus to all around you. Every great idea started with someone coming up with the initial thought.

How can we make a good idea spread? Well I feel the checkerboard system would be the best. If you take a single grain of rice and place it on the first square and then double the number of grains on each following square and keep doubling the amount each time, by the time you arrived at the last square, number sixty-four, you would have enough grains of rice to bury India fifty feet deep. The same goes for making things change. Start with yourself, and then get a friend to join you. Then the two of you get two more, and on it goes. By the way, by the time you get to square number twenty-two, you will be over one million already.

Once you have a large number of you wanting change, then you will want to start cleaning house in all our governmental levels, federal, state and local, and clean out those school board members who will not let Intelligent Design be taught in the school. After a while, the idiots who are trying to take this country down morally and socially will see your train of change coming, and they will run for the hills.

Another thing to do is really lift up those people who have, despite the efforts of the far lefters, continued to stand their ground on what is right and lawful and use that precious thing called common sense in their lives. Also, we need to support and praise those kids today who stand up for Christ and do that gathering around the flagpole each year to pray for their school and country and make a statement of their faith to others. Boys, those are the kind of girls you want to look for as future mates. Girls, the same goes for you when looking for that future husband. Parents, make sure your kids know that you are proud of them being outward with their faith to others, and kids, make sure you keep each other uplifted, as each of you will have one of those days once in a while at school, work, or even possibly at home.

Another person to keep uplifted is your pastor. The new Hate Crimes Bill, passed in 2009, can be a threat to them in the future if someone decides to use it to keep ministers from speaking against the sin of being a gay or lesbian. As your group grows, keep your focus on God, and make your movement responsible to Him for guidance and leading through the Bible. No matter who you are, God has put into our minds that sense of right and wrong. But as with those who want their way only, they are choosing to ignore that sense and let their selfishness take over their lives. They do not want to use common sense, because it interferes with their wants and desires, even if they are detrimental to our nation and people.

So what can we spell with a C? Christ, community, care for others, and most importantly, common sense. We are beyond just asking our Congressional representatives to use it. It is time to start demanding it or we will remove them. Being a Christian does not mean you just sit by and pray that something changes; you have to do something about it, starting with the voting booth.

The Bible tells us in the book of Revelation that there is coming a day when there will be a one-world government (see my book titled *Time Witnessing* for some details on this issue and facts), but until that day comes, we need to keep dealing with these issues that are tearing down our country, denying us our rights to worship God, and trying to prevent Christmas and all that it is about from our public places. When our church choir goes to the local mall to sing Christmas carols, the mall always tells them to not sing anything about Christ or God, but they do anyway. Why? Because it is our right and freedom to express ourselves as we desire, and no authority has the right or ability to deny that freedom. If your local mall will not let you sing Christmas carols about the baby Jesus, Christ, then just start singing outside. The mall is a public place, and they cannot deny you that constitutional right. The same goes for talking to someone about Jesus, being born again, and/or anything about the Bible in a public place. Remember Christ and Christian are both spelled with a C!

Conclusion

A Common-Sense Idea

I am writing this on the Sunday following the 2010 midterm elections. The Republicans took control of the House of Representatives, and the Senate is about as split as it can get, with the Democrats still in the majority. As this next Congress convenes, keep your eyes and ears open and be involved. If you do not know who represents you in Washington DC, go to the House of Representatives' website—www.house.gov—or the Senate website—www.senate.gov. Input your zip code and state name. Both sites will direct you to either your state's senators or your representative for your area of the state.

In 1931, Congress officially made the "Star-Spangled Banner" our national anthem. However, did you know that another song was proposed for that honored place in our country? Just about that time the song "God Bless America" was written by Irving Berlin and performed for the first time. Although not chosen by Congress, it is still one of our most cherished songs and is even sung in place of the national anthem at some sporting events. The Philadelphia Flyers hockey team had Kate Smith's version of the song played at every home game for quite some time, and most recently, singer Celine Dion recorded it to honor those who died on September 11, 2001.

The only reason our country is still free is because God Almighty, not Allah or Buddha or any other false god, has protected and still is protecting us. However, His protection may allow us to suffer judgment if we continue to do all we can to remove God from our nation. The attempts to remove God from our Pledge of Allegiance and our money, the forced removal of the Ten Commandment monuments around the nation, the forcing of cross removals, taking down of the Christian flag, and denying the display of Christmas decorations like nativity scenes will result in God allowing judgment to come upon us as a people and country.

To get this change started, start with yourself. I would challenge you to give serious thought to becoming a Christian and a servant of the only true God. Find a Bible-believing church, and get involved in both the church's outreach and that of our nation. Only in that way will we get this country back on track and giving honor to our protector by praising Him. Read John 3:1–18 (NIV or KJV) in the Bible, and you will learn how much God and His Son, Jesus Christ, love you. Then bow your head and ask Him to come into your heart as your Savior and Lord.

"God bless America!"

Acknowledgement

Special thanks to my nephew, Brett Reichart, his wife Emily, and my wife Lori, for their work and ideas in designing the cover of this book. The use of common sense is definitely on the critical list in this country, and they took my idea and were able to create the characterization for the cover.

Kevin

References

If you made a decision to ask Jesus into your heart through this book, or you are still considering this decision, I would suggest you contact one of the following ministries for guidance and to start your walk with God:

The Billy Graham Evangelistic Association at: www.billygraham.org

InTouch Ministries (Dr. Charles Stanley) at: www.intouch.org

CPSIA information can be obtained at www.ICGtesting.com
261729BV00001B/165/P